Hugh Lofting

Twayne's English Authors Series
Children's Literature

James Gellert, Editor
Lakehead University

TEAS 496

Hugh Lofting, early 1940s. *Reprinted by permission of Christopher Lofting.*

Hugh Lofting

Gary D. Schmidt
Calvin College

Twayne Publishers • New York
Maxwell Macmillan Canada • *Toronto*
Maxwell Macmillan International • *New York   Oxford   Singapore   Sydney*

Twayne's English Authors Series No. 496

Hugh Lofting
Gary D. Schmidt

Twayne Publishers   Maxwell Macmillan Canada, Inc.
Macmillan Publishing Company   1200 Eglinton Avenue East
866 Third Avenue   Suite 200
New York, New York 10022   Don Mills, Ontario M3C 3N1

Library of Congress Cataloging-in-Publication Data
Schmidt, Gary D.
    Hugh Lofting / Gary D. Schmidt.
        p.   cm. -- (Twayne's English authors series. Children's
    literature) (Twayne's English authors series ; TEAS 496)
        Includes bibliographical references and index.
        ISBN 0-8057-7023-2 (alk. paper)
        1. Lofting, Hugh, 1886–1947—Criticism and interpretation.
    2. Children's stories, American—History and criticism.
    3. Dolittle, Doctor (Fictitious character) I. Title. II. Series.
    III. Series: Twayne's English authors series ; TEAS 496.
    PS3523.0335Z87   1992
    813′.52—dc20   92-11256
                                                                         CIP

The paper used in this publication meets the minimum requirements
of American National Standard for Information Sciences—Permanence
of Paper for Printed Library Materials. ANSI Z3948-1984. ♾™

10 9 8 7 6 5 4 3 2 1

Printed in the United States of America

For
Anne
and James, Kathleen, Rebecca, and David—
"More than a trinity of bright messengers"

Contents

Illustrations

Frontispiece

Preface

As a young boy, on a Saturday morning I would walk the four blocks to the Hicksville Public Library (yes, there truly was such a place and it truly was a wonderful library). The Dolittle books were all there, the third shelf up on the fourth set of shelves, a great, bright line of them. Looking back, I suppose they were all rather shabby and dog-earred, but I can remember the feel of them, the excitement they generated, the very smell of the things. I chose them week after week, hoarding them. And I never remember coming to the end of the series, for they all seemed to feed back into one another in a blur of adventures and episodes.

To reread the entire series again now, as an adult literary critic, is to recapture much of the nostalgia of the books. On one level this nostalgia is one of the delights of scholarship in the field of children's literature, for one is reading again the novels and picture books that fed the imagination of one's youth. To pick up a copy of *Doctor Dolittle and the Secret Lake* is to construct an image of the young boy sitting cross-legged on the library floor, scuttled between the shelving, ignoring everything but the story of Mudface.

But this nostalgia is a siren's call, for it has nothing to do with the stuff of literary criticism. If Hugh Lofting is to be considered as a writer of children's literature with any kind of objectivity and sensitivity, then he must be first considered as a writer, and his books as literary texts subject to the questions to which all literary texts are subject. It is not an easy separation, to make the gentle Doctor and the good Stubbins into strangers again. And the reader may find in the following pages that perhaps it is not always possible.

Lofting's reputation has not been untarnished. While the Dolittle books have been praised as children's classics, they have also been labeled as racist. While they have been extolled for their imagination and wit and comedy, they have also been criticized as plodding and predictable. The books have been in and out of print since their beginning 70 years ago, even *The Voyages of Doctor Dolittle,* which is remarkable for a Newbery-winning book. They have been subject to bitter condemnation, editorial changes, truncations, and simple oblivion. It is the basic assumption of this book that Lofting's work needs to be reconsidered, and that that reconsideration needs to be free from all the baggage that has been attached willy-nilly to his books.

For that baggage has shadowed—actually, has completely hidden—the main point of the series: that children need to see examples of kindness and tolerance, of acceptance and gentleness and compassion and understanding. Writing after one world war and in the midst of preparations for another one, Lofting was perhaps one of the few writers of children's literature who saw in his writing a political and moral task: to encourage peace by showing images of peace to the young generation of readers. How successful he was at his task is something that cannot possibly be measured, but there is at least one young reader who loved Dolittle for these qualities, qualities that character maintained in the face of the most amazing adventures.

Lofting dedicated *The Story of Doctor Dolittle* to "All children, children in years and children in heart." It was a dedication that described Lofting's perception of his audience. For Lofting, to be childlike meant being without pretensions, being kind, being close to the natural world, being willing and eager to learn, never posturing, ever yearning to see what lies beyond the seawall. Opposed to this he set images of tin soldiers, adults who lost their childlikeness and, in losing it, became hardened, uncaring, intolerant. If this smacks of didacticism, Lofting would probably not have disagreed. What is remarkable in his writing is that it never seems didactic. The images are woven so completely into the tapestry that it is seamless, of a piece; the plot situations and characterizations themselves give rise to the ethical issues with which Lofting is concerned.

The Dolittle books are sometimes perceived to be old-fashioned. Perhaps they are; they are certainly different from anything being written today in children's literature. That a writer of children's literature would see as one of his central tasks a political endeavor is so remarkable that one can hardly imagine a similar set of books being written. But one would be hard-pressed to find in fantasy today a central concept so simple and yet compelling, a character so simple and yet complex, a narrative strategy so simple and yet effective, a central theme so hopeful and yet not naive.

Acknowledgments

The acknowledgments to this book must begin with those to Hugh Lofting's family, who were all willing to speak about Lofting's work and about his life. I thank Olga Fricker, Lofting's sister-in-law, who contributed to my understanding of Lofting's work on the later books in the Dolittle series. And my thanks go to Christopher Lofting, Colin Lofting, and Elizabeth Lofting Mutrux, who helped me to understand their father's life and its relationship to his work. I am grateful for their permission to quote from and refer to their interviews in the text of this book.

A number of Lofting's minor works are now out of print, and at least one is particularly inaccessible. In tracking down these works, together with innumerable related requests, I am grateful to Conrad Bult, reference librarian of Calvin College Library, and Kathy Struck, also of Calvin College Library. My thanks also to Robert J. Bertholf, curator of the Rare Books Collection of the State University of New York at Buffalo.

My research assistant for this project was Heather Bouwman, and one would be hard-pressed to find anyone more efficient, more thorough. I thank her especially for the sometimes tedious task of hunting down book reviews. That the manuscript was converted from penciled longhand to type is due entirely to her and to the secretary of the English Department, Alma Walhout.

This study was funded in part by a Calvin College Research Fellowship, and my acknowledgment of that carries thanks to the college and my department for their continuing support.

I express my thanks for the following permissions:

From *The Story of Doctor Dolittle* by Hugh Lofting. Copyright 1920 by Hugh Lofting, Centenary Edition © 1988 by Christopher

Lofting. Used by permission of Delacorte Press, a division of Bantam Doubleday Dell Publishing Group, Inc.

From *The Voyages of Doctor Dolittle* by Hugh Lofting. Copyright 1922 by Hugh Lofting, Revised Edition © 1988 by Christopher Lofting. Used by permission of Delacorte Press, a division of Bantam Doubleday Dell Publishing Group, Inc.

From *Doctor Dolittle's Post Office* by Hugh Lofting. Copyright 1923 by Frederick A. Stokes Company, Revised Edition © 1988 by Christopher Lofting. Used by permission of Delacorte Press, a division of Bantam Doubleday Dell Publishing Group, Inc.

From *The Story of Mrs. Tubbs* by Hugh Lofting. Copyright 1923 by Frederick A. Stokes. Used by permission of Christopher Lofting.

From *Doctor Dolittle's Circus* by Hugh Lofting. Copyright 1924 by Frederick A. Stokes Company, Revised Edition © 1988 by Christopher Lofting. Used by permission of Delacorte Press, a division of Bantam Doubleday Dell Publishing Group, Inc.

From *Porridge Poetry* by Hugh Lofting. Copyright 1924 by Frederick A. Stokes. Used by permission of Christopher Lofting.

From *Doctor Dolittle's Zoo* by Hugh Lofting. Copyright 1925 by Frederick A. Stokes. Used by permission of Christopher Lofting.

From *Doctor Dolittle's Caravan* by Hugh Lofting. Copyright 1924, 1925, 1926 by Hugh Lofting, Revised Edition © 1988 by Christopher Lofting. Used by permission of Delacorte Press, a division of Bantam Doubleday Dell Publishing Group, Inc.

From *Doctor Dolittle's Garden* by Hugh Lofting. Copyright 1927 by Frederick A. Stokes Company, Revised Edition © 1988 by Christopher Lofting. Used by permission of Delacorte Press, a division of Bantam Doubleday Dell Publishing Group, Inc.

From *Doctor Dolittle in the Moon* by Hugh Lofting. Copyright 1928 by Frederick A. Stokes, Revised Edition © 1988 by Christopher Lofting. Used by permission of Delacorte Press, a division of Bantam Doubleday Dell Publishing Group, Inc.

From *Noisy Nora: An Almost True Tale* by Hugh Lofting. Copyright 1929 by Frederick A. Stokes. Used by permission of Christopher Lofting.

From *The Twilight of Magic* by Hugh Lofting. Copyright 1930 by Hugh Lofting. Used by permission of Christopher Lofting.

From *Gub Gub's Book* by Hugh Lofting. Copyright 1932 by Hugh Lofting. Used by permission of Christopher Lofting.

From *Doctor Dolittle's Return* by Hugh Lofting. Copyright 1933 by Hugh Lofting, 1961 by Josephine Lofting. Used by permission of Christopher Lofting.

From *Doctor Dolittle's Birthday Book* by Hugh Lofting. Copyright 1935 by Frederick A. Stokes. Used by permission of Christopher Lofting.

From *Tommy, Tilly, and Mrs. Tubbs,* by Hugh Lofting. Copyright 1936 by Frederick A. Stokes. Used by permission of Christopher Lofting.

From *Victory for the Slain* by Hugh Lofting. Copyright 1942 by Hugh Lofting. Used by permission of Christopher Lofting.

From *Doctor Dolittle and the Secret Lake* by Hugh Lofting. Copyright 1923, 1948 by Josephine Lofting. Used by permission of Christopher Lofting.

From *Doctor Dolittle and the Green Canary* by Hugh Lofting. Copyright 1924, 1925, 1950 by Josephine Lofting, Revised Edition © 1988 by Christopher Lofting. Used by permission of Delacorte Press, a division of Bantam Doubleday Dell Publishing Group, Inc.

From *Doctor Dolittle's Puddleby Adventures* by Hugh Lofting. Copyright 1925, 1926, 1950, 1952 by Josephine Lofting. Used by permission of Christopher Lofting.

Finally, I wish to thank Anne, to whom this study is dedicated, for all her many contributions to this project, both seen and unseen. The dedication carries with it all my gratitude and love for her constant encouragement.

Chronology

1886   Hugh John Lofting born in Maidenhead, Berkshire, England, on 14 January to John Brien and Elizabeth Agnes Lofting.

1894   Attends Mount St. Mary's, Chesterfield, Derbyshire.

1904   Attends Massachusetts Institute of Technology.

1906   Returns to England to attend London Polytechnic.

1907   After brief period devoted to architecture, travels to Canada for prospecting and surveying.

1908   Works with Lagos Railway in West Africa and Railways of Havana, Cuba.

1912   Settles in New York and begins writing humorous, burlesque works, short stories, and essays. Marries Flora Small of New York.

1913   Daughter Elizabeth born.

1914   Works for the British Ministry of Information in New York.

1915   Son Colin born.

1916   Joins the British army to serve as captain of the Irish Guards.

1917   Serves for the next two years in Flanders and France.

1918   Is wounded and removed from active duty.

1919   Returns with his family to the United States; meets Cecil Roberts. Family settles in Connecticut; resumes work at British Ministry of Information.

1920   *The Story of Doctor Dolittle.*

1922   *The Voyages of Doctor Dolittle.* Hugh Walpole's enthusiastic preface to the British edition of *The Story of Doctor Dolittle* introduces Dolittle to a British audience.

1923   *Doctor Dolittle's Post Office. The Story of Mrs. Tubbs.* Awarded the Newbery Medal for *The Voyages of Doctor Dolittle.*

1924   *Doctor Dolittle's Circus. Porridge Poetry: Cooked, Ornamented, and Served Up.* "Children and Internationalism" published in the *Nation.*

1925   *Doctor Dolittle's Zoo.*

1926   *Doctor Dolittle's Caravan.*

1927   *Doctor Dolittle's Garden. Doctor Dolittle's Play,* a dramatization by Harcourt Williams, produced in London. Flora Small dies.

1928   *Doctor Dolittle in the Moon.* Marries Katherine Harrower, who dies this same year.

1929   *Noisy Nora.*

1930   *The Twilight of Magic.*

1932   *Gub-Gub's Book: An Encyclopedia of Food in Twenty Volumes.*

1933   *Doctor Dolittle's Return.*

1935   Marries Josephine Fricker of Toronto. Moves to Topanga, California.

1936   *Doctor Dolittle's Birthday Book. Tommy, Tilly, and Mrs. Tubbs.* Son Christopher Clement born.

1942   *Victory for the Slain.*

1947   Dies on 27 September in Santa Monica, California.

1948   *Doctor Dolittle and the Secret Lake.*

1950   *Doctor Dolittle and the Green Canary,* completed by Olga Michael Fricker.

1952   *Doctor Dolittle's Puddleby Adventures,* edited by Josephine Lofting.

1955 Flood in Wilton, Connecticut, destroys some of Lofting's manuscripts owned by Elizabeth Lofting Mutrux.

1967 *Doctor Dolittle: A Treasury,* edited by Olga Fricker. *Doctor Dolittle,* film released by Twentieth Century-Fox Film Corporation.

1988 Dell Publishing Company begins publishing revised versions of eight of the Dolittle novels.

1

From the Trenches of Flanders

The history of children's literature is marked by almost mythical tales of how great classics began under the inspiration of a young child. Beatrix Potter hears of the illness of a young boy and writes *The Tale of Peter Rabbit* to beguile his hours in bed. A. A. Milne begins his Winnie-the-Pooh stories during a rainy holiday season to capture the life of his son. Lewis Carroll composes his *Alice in Wonderland* around the character of Alice Liddell. Richard Adams records the adventures of Hazel and Fiver in *Watership Down* only after using the tales to lull his two daughters to sleep. In each case the tale—in its first version—is produced for a specific audience; only later is it retold for a wider child audience.

So it is with *The Story of Doctor Dolittle,* Hugh Lofting's first and arguably greatest novel. Written from the trenches of World War I, letters about the staid, remarkable Dolittle came to Lofting's two children, Colin and Elizabeth. To the children, those letters became a link to their father; to Lofting, they became a release from the horror that lay so close about. And after he returned home, his letters eventually became the first in a line of novels centered on a character who is one of the most recognizable in children's literature.

It seems remarkable that the character of Doctor Dolittle could come out of the trenches of France and Flanders, yet this kind of opposition characterized Lofting's life, as it characterizes Dolittle's life as well. Lofting, like Dolittle, was self-effacing and quiet, a somewhat dapper fellow who continued to wear spats and, despite many years of life in the United States, never lost his Britishness; in fact, he retained his British citizenship his whole life. He had an intense love of and interest in the animal world, and felt keenly for the suffering of animals. It was this suffering that could bring out aggression from the placid Lofting; once he attacked three men, one armed with a knife, who had hobbled some wild horses. Having dispatched the three, he cut loose the horses, emptied the rifles, and, wiping the blood from his cheek, sauntered back to his camp, unruffled, to read a story to his son.[1] One thinks of Dolittle, who is, infrequently, moved to violence by similar injustices.

At a time when jaded American writers were traveling to Europe to mourn the lost generation, Lofting came to America to take up the task of writing for children. It was as if he unconsciously wished to build contradictions into his life. His works are filled with images of delight and hope, yet the later years of his life were filled with despair and the early years marked by painful tragedy. He wished to become a writer, yet his education was in quite a different sphere. His family life was unutterably important to him, yet he himself grew up with almost none. He was a Victorian who rejected Victorian principles, a man of war who became a man of peace, a writer who blundered into children's literature instead of journalism, his intended area. Finally, he was a man who lived for hope but found that hope was not enough.

Hugh John Lofting was born in 1886, into the very height of the Victorian period. An entire generation of the English had never known anybody but Victoria on the throne. The empire that reached around the globe was racing towards its zenith, and no one guessed that the generation that would be born in this year would be wiped out in muddy, bloody European fields. Despite Darwin and the political consequences of his research, it was an age of optimism; the Crystal Palace was still boasting of the age's success. Britain still ruled the waves, and its heroes were men who fought for the empire: Chinese Gordon had become a martyr only the year before. Perhaps more important for Lofting, though there is not evidence of its importance in his very early childhood, was that a golden age in children's literature was beginning, an age that in some measure ended with the appearance of *The Story of Doctor Dolittle.*

Born in Maidenhead, Berkshire, Lofting was far from the polit-ical life of the Victorian era, but his parentage would have kept him from these circles even if he had desired a political life. Both his father and his mother, John Brien and Elizabeth Agnes Loft-ing, were Roman Catholic. This, together with the fact of John's Irish background, would hardly have propelled him toward the houses of Parliament. He was born into an unsentimental family of six children, where despite inclinations toward becoming a writer—he enjoyed telling stories to his sister and brothers, and one might imagine fireside scenes similar to those of the Dolittle household—he was pushed by his father toward a career in en-gineering, under the presupposition that if a child's career choice should fail, he should at least have a practiced training in a profession.[2] British optimism can go only so far.

Looking back, it is not hard to find in Lofting's childhood the seeds of Doctor Dolittle. Like Dolittle, Lofting loved the natural world; for him, this was manifested in his mountain climbing and fishing trips. He also kept a zoo and a natural history museum in his mother's linen closet, two institutions Dolittle would have as well. Nor is Dolittle's habit of boarding mice in a piano particu-larly different from the linen closet of the young Lofting. (As an adult, Lofting would keep three or four dogs in his home.) And like Dolittle, Lofting yearned to travel and explore, and if his ca-reer in engineering would bring him any satisfaction—and it ap-parently brought very little—it would come in the opportunity to travel.

But Dolittle lay well into the future, unimagined by the young boy who at the age of eight left home, never to live there fully again. Though in later life they were closer—Elizabeth Lofting remembering her grandfather as "very quiet" and her grand-mother as "very sympathetic"—at this time in his childhood Loft-

ing had only infrequent contact with his parents.[3] (Perhaps it is
not hard to imagine why there is so little family life in the Dolittle
novels, or why there is not a single true motherly figure.) He traveled to Mount St. Mary's, a Jesuit school in Chesterfield, Derbyshire, where he received a classical Catholic education, learning
Latin and Greek. Here he resolved to become a civil engineer, sat-
isfying the demands of his father and the inclinations of his own
heart, for such a career would call for traveling.

Lofting was to remain at Mount St. Mary's for 10 years, and if
the reminiscences of Father James Scholes, a schoolfellow, are
accurate, it was a time of almost complete isolation:

> It was rather like a very large family (120 boys), strict in
> religious observance, not very interested in the world
> outside but absorbed with its own activities, joys and sor-
> rows. The School was almost the entire boy's life, and the
> staff had very little interest beside the good of the boys
> spiritually, morally and educationally; they devoted
> their time not merely to the betterment of the boys but
> also to seeing that their lives were punctuated by out-
> ings, special days, and especially plays and concerts. A
> boy was in fact brought up in an atmosphere almost im-
> possible to communicate to others, and which I can
> glimpse only by constant contact with one or two who
> were brought up under this paternalistic and devoted
> treatment.[4]

Lofting never wrote of his school life and the sheltering devotion
of the institution. Certainly none of the children in his novels experience anything like it. Perhaps glimpses of it may be caught
in Dolittle's enclosed garden, whose walls effectively cut him off
from the meddlesome outside world. But at the conclusion of 10
years, Lofting had had enough of shelter.

In 1904 he began the first of many travels as he crossed the
ocean and enrolled at the Massachusetts Institute of Technology,
where he took courses in civil engineering, with an emphasis on
architecture. He remained in Cambridge only a year and then

returned to England to finish his degree in 1907 at the London Polytechnic. This rapid movement back and forth across oceans would mark his life for the next five years until he resolved upon his true career. After his graduation he traveled west again and spent two years surveying and prospecting in Canada—perhaps not the career his father would have hoped for. From 1908 to 1912 he fulfilled his early ambition to explore (one sees here the seeds of Tommy Stubbins sitting on the seawall). He journeyed to West Africa (where Dolittle too would journey) to work for Lagos Railways. Then he traveled west again to Cuba, here to work for Railways of Havana.

It cannot have been an easy period for Lofting. Certainly he was fulfilling the romantic dream of voyaging to distant places, and one senses that the delight that both Stubbins and Dolittle feel as they resolve upon a voyage must be akin to that which Lofting himself felt. But the tension lay in oppositions, as they would all of his life. He enjoyed the trips his profession called for, yet he considered himself to be a bad engineer (there is no evidence that this is so) and disliked his tasks. In addition, he could not escape his identification with other Englishmen who heeded Kipling's advice and set forth from the cliffs of England to bring civilization. He would despise the arrogant imperialism of the period, yet could not help but be colored by it. The tension ended in 1912 when Lofting turned to the profession least likely to suit the demands of his father: he became a writer.

In that year Lofting moved to New York, married Flora Small, and abandoned the profession of engineering. He would never give up his British citizenship, and would remain "terribly British," but, Christopher Lofting remembers, he would nevertheless develop a strong loyalty for the United States.[5] Now he was 26 years old and ready to turn to writing and storytelling, his childhood interest. It was not a completely new direction for him; as a student he had written short plays and stories. But ensconced in New York, the center of America's literary effort, Lofting took on the role of the writer, centering his efforts on adult literature. He wrote burlesques and comedies, marked by puns and broad humor. And he wrote press articles, so that had international events taken different turns, Lofting might have become a journalist. Instead, what Lofting would later ironically call another war to end all wars brought him back across the ocean yet again.

At the outbreak of the war, Lofting worked for the British Ministry of Information in New York. But in 1916, a year after the birth of the Loftings' first son, Lofting enlisted in the British army. For the next two years Lofting served as a captain of the Irish Guards in Flanders and France, experiencing all the horrors of trench warfare: the rot of the trenches, the floods of green gas, the brutalization of those living creatures around him, the senseless loss of life to gain a few yards of bloodied earth. The almost unspeakable horror of these years must have been nearly overwhelming, but for the simple request from Lofting's two children, Colin and Elizabeth, that he write letters home telling them stories. It must have seemed to Lofting that he was replaying his own childhood.

Years later, writing for *The Book of Junior Authors,* Lofting described the genesis of Doctor Dolittle:

> It was during the Great War and my children at home wanted letters from me—and they wanted them with illustrations rather than without. There seemed very little of interest to write to youngsters from the Front: the news was either too horrible or too dull. And it was all censored. One thing, however, that kept forcing itself more and more on my attention was the very considerable part the animals were playing in the World War and that as time went on they, too, seemed to become Fatalists. They took their chances with the rest of us. But their fate was far different from the men's. However seriously a soldier was wounded, his life was not despaired of; all the resources of a surgery highly developed by the war were brought to his aid. A seriously wounded horse was put out by a timely bullet.
>
> This did not seem quite fair. If we made the animals take the same chances as we did ourselves, why did we not give them similar attention when wounded? But ob-

viously to develop a horse-surgery as that of our Casualty Clearing Stations would necessitate a knowledge of horse language.

That was the beginning of the idea: an eccentric country physician with a bent for natural history and a great love of pets, who finally decides to give up his human practice for the more difficult, more sincere and, for him, more attractive therapy of the animal kingdom. He is challenged by the difficulty of the work—for obviously it requires a much cleverer brain to become a good animal doctor (who must first acquire all animal languages and physiologies) than it does to take care of the mere human hypochondriac.

This was a new plot for my narrative letter for the children. It delighted them.[6]

The equation of animal life with human life seems a bit curious but discloses a sensibility that is akin to Dolittle himself, who consistently resists assigning relative values to lives. The notion that a horse surgery would require a knowledge of horse language is the imaginative leap of the storyteller. It would provide the core idea of the Dolittle novels.

In 1918 Lofting was wounded in the upper thigh, struck by a piece of shrapnel from a hand grenade. (The piece was never removed and in later years caused him some trouble with phlebitis.)[7] Soon after he was removed from active duty. Flora left the children in New York with a nurse and traveled to Britain; the children joined their parents when the war ended.[8] In the autumn of 1919 Lofting, together with his family, boarded ship to return to the United States; although he would continue to travel, he would never live anywhere else again. He brought with him the letters that he had written and that had indeed delighted his children. Colin had been so enchanted that he adopted "Dolittle" as a nickname, perhaps appropriately, given that his snub nose was so like that of Dolittle himself.

The crossing was a fortuitous one, for on it Lofting met Cecil Roberts, a minor British novelist and editor whose works today are forgotten but whose name must be always footnoted to an account of Lofting's life. When he found that Lofting had written some stories for his children, he asked to read them and was impressed by their quality. With the encouragement of Flora, Lofting was by this time already wondering if the stories could make a book, and Roberts encouraged him, suggesting that Lofting contact a publisher, Frederick A. Stokes Company of New York, the firm with which Roberts would publish during the next decade. This Lofting did, beginning a long relationship with the firm and with Helen Dean Fish as his editor. Though he was to write some short pieces and one long narrative poem for an adult audience, his writing career was from this moment on channeled into the field of children's literature.

The family settled into a succession of homes in Connecticut. In Wilmot they chose an 1835 farmhouse on Chestnut Hill Road, locally known as the Kellogg House. Here, in a two-story barn that overlooked fields and woods, Lofting wrote *The Voyages of Doctor Dolittle.* (A little less than three decades later, Robert Lawson would write another Newbery Medal–winner near this house: *Rabbit Hill.*) They then moved to the Ewing House on Olmstead Hill Road in Wilton, and from there to a house known as Stony Brook in Westport.

The family was moving farther and farther east, until finally they chose a home in Madison, Connecticut, a small town on the coast of Long Island Sound, not too close to the city but not too far from the publishing house. Lofting's parents had by this time become quite proud of their son's work, and came on at least one occasion to visit the family while they lived in Madison.[9] Here was written the great flood of the Dolittle's, a flood so remarkable that it must have astonished his publishers. Stokes had immediately accepted *The Story of Doctor Dolittle,* and it was published in 1920. Its enthusiastic reception by reviewers and readers encouraged Lofting, and when a highly laudatory preface by Hugh Walpole was added to the British edition in 1922—Walpole claimed it as a new classic—he gained an additional audience in England. In that same year Stokes would publish *The Voyages of Doctor Dolittle,* which in 1923 garnered Lofting his single award in children's literature: the Newbery Medal. *Doctor Dolittle's Post Office* would follow in 1923, and from there *Doctor Dolittle's Circus* (1924), *Doctor Dolittle's Zoo* (1925), *Doctor Dolittle's Caravan* (1926), *Doctor Dolittle's Garden* (1927), and *Doctor Dolittle in the Moon* (1928)—a goodly procession. It was as if Lofting at age 34 had finally found himself and had begun to harvest the bounty of stories that grew so richly in his imagination. The stories were never conceived as oral tales, but instead he took them down in pencil on yellow legal pads, writing in two columns. The books themselves, enormous books to be written so quickly, strain at their seams under the pressure of the sheer number of stories that are packed in. This is all the more remarkable when we consider that Lofting spent a great deal of time in this decade visiting schools and children's organizations and talking to children and librarians.

Flora was not to see the last of this succession; she died in 1927. Other than her enouragement of the first novel, Lofting never recorded her reaction to the books, or how she might have supported him in his writing. Certainly her death was one of the factors in the end of that wild careening of words. Christopher Lofting suggests as well that Lofting was tired of Dolittle and sent him to the moon to be rid of him, though the ending of that novel certainly leaves open the possibility of a sequel.[10] Of all the Dolittle books, *Doctor Dolittle in the Moon* is one of those most clearly meant to have a sequel. In any case Lofting's work must have been interrupted by yet another tragedy. In 1928, only a few months after he married Katherine Harrower, she was infected in an epidemic of influenza and died as well. The next Dolittle book, *Doctor Dolittle's Return,* would not be issued for five years. The next, *Doctor Dolittle and the Secret Lake,* would take 13 years.

This gap might also be accounted for by another cause: Lofting chaffed at the idea of being labeled as an author of juvenile books; he yearned to write and publish an adult novel, Christopher Lofting recalls. But his publisher and audience claimed his attention and pressured him to continue the Dolittle series. For Lofting, *Doctor Dolittle and the Secret Lake* was a compromise, for he saw it as an adult book but one within the context and imaginative framework of the Dolittle characters. The book "represents a man trying to get away from children's literature," argues Christopher Lofting, and this accounts at least in part for the book's much more serious tone.[11]

The Dolittle books would reflect Lofting's concern with issues of peace and justice, but they were not the only forums in which he addressed those issues. In 1924 he wrote an article for the *Nation* entitled "Children and Internationalism." "It would not be too much to assert that recently there has been hardly anyone— of those who give thought at all to public affairs—who has not experienced a lurking suspicion that we're not going to get any- where until we face this question of nationalism vs. internation- alism," he begins.[12] The sometimes bitter article is an attack on what Lofting calls "tin-soldierism," a parochial state of mind that insists on glorifying war and battle and the brave charges for he- roic deaths. This is a mind-set that he sometimes attacks in the Dolittle novels and that he deplores in children's literature:

> The boy may not have heard his father boasting of the
> glories of a crack regiment, but he has read a whole heap
> of so-called Children's Classics in which highly painted
> heroes galloped, glorious and victorious, across bloody
> battlefields. That kind of battlefield has gone for good—
> it is still bloody, but you don't gallop. And since that kind
> of battlefield has gone, that kind of book—for children—
> should go too.

One cannot help but hear Lofting's trench experience here; he had seen firsthand the bloody fields and the glorious but futile charges over the top. This argument leads Lofting to conclude that all children's works that glorify war and violence in the name of country should be eliminated.

Throughout the essay, Lofting is most interested in the next generation: "If, beginning with the children, we launch a cam- paign for the right kind of Peace Preparedness, the working out of governmental plans later will be easier." The lack of this preparedness is precisely what he will lament in "Victory for the Slain"; instead, he will note in that poem, tin-soldierdom will remain. And so the essay's concluding call for "mutual tolerance and undisturbed self-expression" versus blind patriotism (he calls the claim "my country right or wrong" "that terrible phrase") was to fall on deaf ears, uttered as it was in a decade marked by an exuberant celebration of the nation's newfound place of strength in the world community.

As the decade turned and Lofting moved into the 1930s, he found himself a successful author in children's literature but a Cassandra in world affairs. In the early part of the decade, the Great Depression had settled on the country and Germany had begun its movement to militarization. The history of the decade would be a repudiation of Lofting's internationalism, and his later work reflects a growing despondency and even a sense of futility.

But in the middle of the decade, Lofting met someone who was to hold back the tide of discouragement for a time, Josephine Fricker. He met her while on a lecture tour in Toronto, and in 1935 they married and moved to Topanga, California. The next year their only child, Christopher Clement, was born. It was to be a happy time for Lofting, and his new family, together with the encouragement of his readership and the editorial and secretarial assistance of Josephine's sister Olga Michael Fricker, led him to begin to forge *Doctor Dolittle's Secret Lake,* perhaps the darkest in tone of all the Dolittle novels.

It was a hard writing for him. Distressed by his old war wounds, perhaps still suffering from the severe ulcers that had beset him in his early forties, he did not write at the pace he was once able to sustain. Olga Michael Fricker recalls that during the writing he was confined to his bed; the slow pace of the work was enormously frustrating for him, though even here his definition of "slow pace" was the rewriting of a chapter every two days.[13]

He interrupted the writing in the summer of 1941 to compose a passionate, despairing poem on the recurrence and futility of war in human history, a poem whose title—"Victory for the Slain"—bears witness to his own grim vision of humanity, a vision that grew grimmer as he grew older. In that summer he confided to friends that if the poem were not finished and published by the end of the year, it would not then be published by an American publisher, for by that time the country would be at war with Japan.[14] Here too he seemed to be a Cassandra, but here he was validated. Despite American optimism, the country did enter into war at the year's end, and the poem was not accepted, given the militant atmosphere of the times. The poem was accepted by Jonathan Cape, Lofting's British publisher. It came out in 1942.

Lofting lived to complete the manuscript of *Doctor Dolittle's Secret Lake* but did not see its publication. Having dedicated the book to his son Christopher, whom he had known for only 11 years, he died in his Santa Monica home in September 1947. Colin Lofting recalls a complete physical failure that seems to have involved his liver and some form of cancer.[15] But given the state of the world then, it is not hard to imagine that he died of a broken heart.

Edward Blishen has suggested that Lofting was characterized by an "essentially reserved nature."[16] G. Wren Howard, his British publisher, remembered him as "rather quiet and shy, shut up inside himself." Olga Michael Fricker, his sister-in-law, recalls his "charm and whimsy."[17] To Lois Lenski, he was "a dignified Englishman," remarkable for one who had lived most of his life in the United States.[18] To his readers, though, Lofting will always seem a bit like the gentle Doctor he created. Or perhaps a bit like Tommy Stubbins, who looked out from the seawall to a world of infinite possibility, of marvelous adventures, and of disturbed peace.

2

The Story of Doctor Dolittle and *The Voyages of Doctor Dolittle*:
The Repudiation of Eden

The tale of the origin of *The Story of Doctor Dolittle* has that sort of mythical quality about it which suggests that, even had it not happened this way, it certainly should have. Hugh Lofting, huddling in the mud and ooze of the World War I trenches, looks about him and sees death and cruelty in the most violent forms. While he could somehow avoid despair and place the war in the context of a reasonable explanation—these were apparently rational creatures who had consciously decided to commit atrocity— he could not accept the destruction of the horses. While the troops could protect themselves against the green gas that poured into the trenches and coated the landscape, the horses could not. It sprang into their lungs, blistered their tissues, and led to agonizing death.

It was to expiate this vision and to respond to the demands of Colin and Elizabeth that Lofting began to write letters back to his family of a gentler time, a gentler place. Set in the small village of Puddleby-on-the-Marsh at the beginning of Victoria's reign, the action of these letters and, later, *The Story of Doctor Dolittle* denies (seemingly) the possibility of a world like that of the trenches. These horses are fitted with glasses rather than slaughtered, and the animal kingdom is given a certain validity: it is a worthwhile endeavor to doctor animals. In fact, though this is only hinted at in the opening novels, that doctoring and its implicit assumption of the worth and value of the animal world become a metaphor for Lofting's vision of what humanity ought to be.

The fact of a writer beginning a work of children's literature with a letter or set of tales to a child has a number of analogies in British literature, so much so that it has virtually become a topos in itself. What distinguishes Lofting from other writers within this group is that while Potter and Grahame created their stories to beguile a child, Lofting endowed his stories with a therapeutic role aimed principally at himself and a generation of children. It is that aspect of these stories which prevents their sense of "oughtness" from being reduced to moral didacticism, for regardless of how serious the matter of the novels becomes, it is always couched in gentle fantasy and witty comedy. This comic context establishes the character of Doctor Dolittle and sets the boundaries within which the action of each of the 12 novels takes place. And yet that context was ultimately not sufficient to overcome the vision of the trenches, the belief that humanity is, in the end, capable of incredible evil. This would lead finally to a rejection of the kind of Eden that Victorian and Edwardian writers of children's literature had tried to create by riverbanks and hedgerows and lettuce gardens and 100-Akre woods. For Lofting, Eden too was a war casualty.

The Story of Doctor Dolittle

Rarely has a children's novel been published with the kind of praise that *The Story of Doctor Dolittle* received. In 1922 Hugh Walpole wrote a preface to the first British edition, where he extravagantly suggested that the book "was a work of genius, and as always with works of genius, it is difficult to analyze the elements that have gone to make it. . . . I don't know how Mr. Lofting has done it: I don't suppose that he knows himself. There it is—the first real children's classic since *Alice*."[1] Here he was echoing a review that came out that same year in the *Nation,* where Mabel Mussey noted that "[f]or more than half a century Alice has ruled supreme in Wonderland. How glad she must be to make room on her throne for the genial animal-doctor, a man after her own heart, and his remarkable household."[2] More immediately, the reviewer for the *New York Times Book Review* characterized the new novel as "strange," "fascinating," "queer," "wondrous," "most whimsical," and "most amusing," suggesting that the reviewer did not quite know what to make of the book, though the critic concluded that this is "a book to greet with delight, to cherish, and if to lend, then gone for good."[3] Anne Carroll Moore argued in the *Bookman* that the novel was "the most delightful nonsense story of the year,"[4] and the reviewer for the *Literary Digest* reveled in "the delightful sense of proportion in his [Lofting's] imagination."[5] There was nary a dissenting voice.

Later critics have tempered their voices only slightly. "*The Story of Doctor Dolittle* must rank at least among the dozen best children's books," writes Roger Lancelyn Green. "[T]here is a 'fine careless rapture' about this which is dipped in the true magic of inspired fantasy."[6] Margaret Blount claimed that "[s]omething quite dazzlingly new and simple is what *The Story of Doctor Dolittle* is. The first moment of human-animal communication in human terms of words and grammar is as strange and marvellous as the animals giving strength to Arthur's arm when he pulls the Sword from the Stone."[7] Helen Dean Fish wrote that "Doctor Dolittle is a good man for children to know because he stands for kindliness, patience and reliability, mixed with delightful humor, energy and gaiety, a combination rarely met and hard to beat."[8] Edward Blishen was closest to a more objective appraisal: "Lofting was, in a literary sense, a fortunate man. His first book was founded on an invention that is not merely ingenious (and one he had the gift to build on, for much of a writing lifetime) but that also enabled him to express what he wished to say about the world, without stint or dilution or camouflage, to the very audience to whom he thought it most worth saying."[9] In examining the Dolittle series as a series, it is Blishen's comment that is most striking: Lofting was able to assert philosophical and ethical positions by placing them within the imaginative and fantastic context of the adventures of a man who could talk to animals in such a way as to destroy neither the tone of the fantasy nor the impact of the message. Perhaps not until Natalie Babbitt's *Tuck Everlasting,* or perhaps Lloyd Alexander's *The High King,* would a novelist of children's literature walk this tenuous tightrope with such ease and grace.

The Story of Doctor Dolittle begins with an affirmation as remote in time and setting as any folktale: "Once upon a time, many years ago—when our grandfathers were little children—there was a doctor; and his name was Dolittle."[10] The accompanying illustration places the reader high above the town of Puddleby-on-the-Marsh, looking down on a neat and orderly Victorian street. Except for the cat, startled by the reader's intrusion, all is calm and peaceful.

But this peace is shattered early on in the story when Dolittle begins accumulating pets; eventually the animals drive away the doctor's human patients, to his sister's chagrin. She is principally worried about finances, something that is merely bothersome for the doctor. When Polynesia, the Doctor's parrot, teaches him how to speak various animal languages, the doctor abandons his human practice and becomes a veterinarian. Since he can communicate directly with animals—and since he is, above all, a kind man—he becomes beloved throughout the animal world.

For a time his animal practice ends his difficulties with money. But eventually the sheer number of pets and the presence of a crocodile that frightens off paying clients leads again to poverty, and this time Sarah Dolittle abandons him. "'All right,' said the Doctor, 'go and get married. It can't be helped.' And he took down his hat and went out into the garden" (22–23), confirming his bachelorhood and rejection of conventional modes of living. The family he will ultimately gain is to be quite different from anything Sarah could have imagined.

Immediately afterward Dolittle receives a message from Africa: the monkeys are dying from an undefined sickness. Though he has no money, Dolittle is able to borrow a ship from a sailor and he and several animals embark on the first of many voyages they will undertake. Guided by a swallow, flying fish, and porpoises, they reach Africa, though their ship is wrecked on the coast. All

"A little town called Puddleby-on-the-Marsh"

Reprinted from *The Story of Doctor Dolittle* (frontispiece) by Hugh Lofting. Copyright 1920 by Hugh Lofting, Centenary Edition © 1988 by Christopher Lofting. Used by permission of Delacorte Press, a division of Bantam Doubleday Dell Publishing Group, Inc.

17

of Dolittle's companions—Jip the dog, Dab-Dab the duck, Polynesia the parrot, Gub-Gub the pig, Chee-Chee the monkey, Too-
Too the owl—are saved from the shipwreck.

Once onshore, they are imprisoned by a tribe that has been
cheated by an ivory hunter. They escape from the prison when
Polynesia frightens the king into releasing them, though soon
once again they are chased by the king's men. Saved by a group
of monkeys, Dolittle eventually sets up a hospital, elicits the cooperation of other animals in running the wards, and cures the
monkeys. As a reward the Doctor is given the rarest animal of all:
the two-headed pushmi-pullyu. On the way back to the coast, Dolittle's party is again caught and imprisoned. They escape this
time when Dolittle turns Prince Bumpo's face white in exchange
for Dolittle's freedom and a boat. Chee-Chee, Polynesia, and the
crocodile are left behind in their native Africa, "and after they had
called Good-by to him again and again and again, they still stood
there upon the rocks, crying bitterly and waving till the ship was
out of sight" (110).

On the way home Dolittle outwits a group of pirates: he takes
their ship (his own having sunk because of its poor construction)
and turns the pirates into birdseed farmers. He also rescues a
young boy from their hold, and then, guided only by Jip's extraordinary sense of smell, he also rescues the boy's uncle, who is
stranded on an island. For this, Jip is given a solid-gold collar.
The party returns home and shows the pushmi-pullyu at side-
shows. The money from this—together with that on the pirate
ship—allows the Doctor to return to Puddleby financially secure.

The sheer fecundity of the adventures leaves the reader breathless. Dolittle is never in one setting for more than a few chapters;
his journey on the sea becomes a string of quickly paced episodes.
Yet there is no restlessness about him—that will come in the sequel to *The Story of Doctor Dolittle*. There is instead an almost
frenzied rushing about from adventure to adventure, all set in the
context of self-assured security. And though these adventures are
more potentially dangerous than those in which A. A. Milne
would set his characters, there is the sense that Lofting is playing

the role of Christopher Robin in this book, and that 100-Akre Wood is not very far from Puddleby-on-the-Marsh.

For in the same way that the plots of the *Winnie-the-Pooh* books were ostensibly directed by the imagination of a child, so are the adventures of *The Story of Doctor Dolittle* organized around the kind of story a child would create, in a world a child would create. The strength of this childlike imagination seems to grow in influence through the course of the plot as the reader moves from the domestic difficulties of a brother and sister living in a small English village, to a ship wrecked on the coast of Africa, to an African village where Dolittle and his party are imprisoned, to pirates, and on and on until the journey ends and the Doctor returns to Puddleby. One might almost be in Peter Pan's Neverland.

The settings here are the exotic ones a child—particularly a Victorian child, growing up in the context of a culture that defined itself as an empire—would choose. Africa, pirate ships, seemingly deserted islands, the Land of the Monkeys—these are the expected settings of the childlike imagination. What prevents Lofting from just working with clichés, however, is the character of Dolittle himself. He is the exact opposite of the kind of protagonist one might expect in these settings. The absolute antithesis of Allan Quartermain, Dolittle subverts all expectations that Lofting's exotic settings might establish.

For in *The Story of Doctor Dolittle* (though not in the later novels), Dolittle is a child. He carries the same levels of responsibility and the same sense of respectability that a child might have. One of the first illustrations of Dolittle pictures him sitting on the wall, by his garden, his feet dangling over the edge. The picture recalls that of Tommy Stubbins in *The Voyages of Doctor Dolittle*; he too dangles his legs over the wall and looks out at the world. Both, in that moment, have the carefree abandon of the child.

The adult kinds of concerns that one might expect of a country veterinarian have no place in Dolittle's world. Though there are recurring questions about money and financial security, they are meaningless questions because, for the most part, they are irrel-

"They came at once to his house on the edge of the town"

Reprinted from *The Story of Doctor Dolittle* (15) by Hugh Lofting. Copyright 1920 by Hugh Lofting, Centenary Edition © 1988 by Christopher Lofting. Used by permission of Delacorte Press, a division of Bantam Doubleday Dell Publishing Group, Inc.

evant to the context in which Dolittle operates. Money is a bothersome trifle, one Dolittle is generally able to do without. Like Pooh, who may always expect that a pot of honey will be ever available, Dolittle expects that things will go along without too much concern for finances. And in the end he is right: he returns to his home financially secure not so much because of the proceeds from his carnival attraction as from the expected intervention of an author who will make all things well.

A large part of the reason for Dolittle's lack of concern is his enormous optimism, his complete confidence that things will turn out all right. When he first learns that the monkeys in Africa are dying, he faces the problem of getting there:

> "I would gladly go to Africa—especially in this bitter weather. But I'm afraid we haven't money enough to buy the tickets. Get me the money-box, Chee-Chee."
>
> So the monkey climbed up and got it off the top shelf of the dresser.
>
> There was nothing in it—not one single penny!
>
> "I felt sure there was twopence left," said the Doctor.
>
> "There *was,*" said the owl. "But you spent it on a rattle for that badger's baby when he was teething."
>
> "Did I?" said the Doctor—"dear me, dear me! What a nuisance money is, to be sure! Well, never mind. Perhaps if I go down to the seaside I shall be able to borrow a boat that will take us to Africa. I knew a seaman once who brought his baby to me with measles. Maybe he'll lend us his boat—the baby got well."
>
> So early the next morning the Doctor went down to the seashore. And when he came back he told the animals it was all right—the sailor was going to lend them the boat. (30–32)

This passage is remarkable in its tone, for Dolittle actually is denying the reality of the circumstances that prohibit his going. He looks in a can for twopence, as though that would help. He naively assumes that a sailor would lend him a boat to go to Africa. Despite the apparent hopelessness of this, the tone is not forlorn, not desperate. It is an assured tone, and in fact everything does turn out. The conclusion—"the sailor was going to lend them his boat"—is understated, as though there is nothing unusual in this event. And, in fact, in the world of Doctor Dolittle it is not unusual.

This irresponsible optimism—the stuff of childhood—is combined with an inordinate gentleness and amiability. These latter qualities establish the character of Dolittle and determine the ways in which he reacts to various adventures. He travels to the heart of a continent, observes the Bridge of Apes (the reader is told that the monkeys had "never let a white man get a glimpse of it before" [64]), and does something as innocuous as set up a hospital. He is trapped by Africans and tricks them for an escape. He meets a set of fierce pirates and maroons them on an island not to suffer but to become birdseed farmers. In each case he avoids the expected directions of action that a protagonist in this setting and in this plot situation might be expected to take. If he is a child, he is a gentle one, who cares for those in his adventures as surely as he himself is cared for by the hand of the author.

Rarely has there been a book so often praised for the wrong reasons. Those critics who do deal with the Dolittle books generally focus on the character of the Doctor while ignoring the context that establishes that character. E. H. Colwell's laudatory comments are typical:

> Doctor Dolittle is a remarkable man, a scientist who spends his life in careful experiments and research. He lived in 1839 when there was still much to discover and he takes his discoveries so seriously that we must too. His interests lead him far afield into many dangers which make excellent material for exciting stories. Whatever the danger, the little man remains calm, and however awkward the situation he always retains his top hat and little bag. He is a born reformer and speaks out fearlessly whatever the danger to himself. "Why don't you have windows in your prisons, you black-faced ruf-

fian," he says hotly—scarcely the best way to placate his jailor! He is unworldly and incurably generous, so that to acquire any money is merely an excuse for spending it on some helpless animal. "What a nuisance money is, to be sure!" he says mildly when Dab-Dab, his housekeeper, asks for money for household expenses. His great sense of duty and unselfishness calls forth the affection of his friends, human and animal, who unite to protect him from the results of his own kindness. Doctor Dolittle is certainly Hugh Lofting's masterpiece, and because we cannot but believe in him we accept the animals who surround him also.[11]

In fact, much of this is simply not the case. Readers are not intended to take his discoveries seriously—this is the stuff of fantasy; what the reader is to note is Dolittle's unrestricted enthusiasm for his experiments. Dolittle does not always remain calm—to do so would be inappropriate in the plot settings Lofting establishes. What is true is that while Dolittle will often respond dramatically to events, he will at all times remain unperturbed and in control. He is not unworldly and is often concerned with money, but that concern is consistently nullified by the pressures of the moment and the Doctor's self-assurance.

When Colwell writes that "because we cannot but believe in him [the Doctor] we accept the animals who surround him also," he misunderstands the nature of the fantasy. The reader may suspend disbelief and thus accept the Doctor and the animals in the context of their adventures, but one does not, at least in *The Story of Doctor Dolittle,* come to believe in the character of Doctor Dolittle as a credible personality. The Doctor is accepted in this first novel because he is a projection of the child's imagination. Cloaked as an adult and thus freed from some of the restrictions an Edwardian child would face, Dolittle acts out in a gentle manner the imaginative exploits of a child. It is this element of Dolittle that leads to the establishment of his character.

At the same time, Colwell's description of Dolittle's character does approach a strong concern of the Dolittle series, a concern

mostly hinted at in the first novel: Dolittle's vision of the nature
of the world about him. Dolittle rejects fame in his own society
and instead chooses a different kind of life: that of a country vet.
The result is that he is rewarded with greater fame, but in another sphere:

> And so, in a few years' time, every living thing for miles
> and miles got to know about John Dolittle, M.D. And the
> birds who flew to other countries in the winter told the
> animals in foreign lands of the wonderful doctor of Pud-
> dleby-on-the-Marsh, who could understand their talk
> and help them in their troubles. In this way he became
> famous among the animals—all over the world—better
> known even than he had been among the folks of the
> West Country. And he was happy and liked his life very
> much. (16–17)

It is the nature of this sphere and Dolittle's engagement with it
that suggest Dolittle's—and Lofting's—own perceptions about the
world. Dolittle's animal world is a gentle world: the horse in need
of glasses kicks an offending boy "in the right place" (14). It is
characterized by loyalty, perseverance, fortitude, justice, and concern. The closed sphere of Dolittle's own animal family, which is
itself characterized by nothing short of familial love, is extended
outward to include all the world, so that Dolittle's family rescues
not only members of the animal world (like the stricken monkeys)
but also human beings (the sailor marooned on a barren island).
This kind of universal concern was to be sharpened and defined
more acutely in the subsequent novels, so that even Lofting's last
fully formed novel, *Doctor Dolittle and the Secret Lake,* reflects
precisely this same concern, though with a much more serious
tone.

It is this gentle concern of Dolittle that motivates the action of
the plot. The journey is undertaken to rescue the monkeys of Africa, and the subsequent adventures all fall within the context of
this journey. Most of the adventures are caused by human beings
who function as blocking elements to Dolittle's journey and mission: the king and queen of the Jolloginki, Prince Bumpo, the pi-

rates. Each is overcome with the aid of the animal world, subverting the kinds of human-animal relationships suggested at the opening of the novel.

The closing of the novel suggests another issue that would be developed later in the series—the notion of story: "And when winter came again, and the snow flew against the kitchen-window, the Doctor and his animals would sit round the big, warm fire after supper; and he would read aloud to them out of his books" (179). The homey image—one that would be repeated in later novels—shows a concern for narrative as a way of entertaining. But the notion of story is also mirrored in the tales generated about Dolittle himself. The concluding passage dramatically shifts the scene from the cozy kitchen to Africa:

> But far away in Africa, where the monkeys chattered in the palm-trees before they went to bed under the big yellow moon, they would say to one another,
>
> "I wonder what The Good Man's doing now—over there, in the Land of the White men! Do you think he ever will come back?"
>
> And Polynesia would squeak out from the vines,
>
> "I think he will—I guess he will—I hope he will!"
>
> And then the crocodile would grunt up at them from the black mud of the river,
>
> "I'm SURE he will—Go to sleep!" (179–80)

Suddenly Dolittle himself has become the subject of narrative, as he has been all along for the reader. In addition to the strong suggestion that this is not the end of the story of Doctor Dolittle (a fact emphasized by the final illustration, in which the Doctor's hand blots out the concluding letter of "END"), there is the supposition that story itself is important, that story establishes memory. The exploration of the meaning of story is deepened in *The Voyages of Doctor Dolittle,* and it becomes one of the primary foci of the later novels.

There would not be another book like *The Story of Doctor Dolittle* in the rest of the Dolittle series. It seems almost as if the first novel had been the development of the conception of the character of Dolittle, while the rest worked out that character's ability to carry the thematic weight of Lofting's philosophical positions. Blishen suggests that the major difference between the first two books is that the first sounds like the amusing uncle talking down to the audience of children; the whole business is something of a benign joke. The second has none of the jokelike quality about it but is meant to be taken much more seriously, though still as a fantasy.[12] This is a metaphoric way of suggesting, in reality, that once the narrator changes, the entire tone of the series changes, so that even when Stubbins is not narrating one of the later books, that book still does not revert back to the narrator of *The Story of Doctor Dolittle*.

And suddenly, once the reader is looking through Stubbins's eyes, Dolittle himself is no longer the caricature, the fumbling but lovable eccentric, the chubby and rounded baby-cum-adult. He is a great and renowned scientist, worthy of respect and, at first from Tommy, even awe. The illustrations themselves attest to this, as the Dolittle of *The Story of Doctor Dolittle* (whose nose, at least, was founded on that of Colin) changes from a dumpy, almost grotesquely caricatured figure whose limbs are always misproportioned and whose face seems made of dough into the familiar, simply lined figure who remains comic but who bears himself with a calm dignity. The change in perception is a masterstroke, the one change that allowed Lofting to go on for 10 more novels without losing completely a framework for the imaginative adventures of the character.

The Voyages of Doctor Dolittle

The movement from *The Story of Doctor Dolittle* to *The Voyages of Doctor Dolittle* is almost a movement between genres. Wolfgang Schlegelmilch has argued that the difference in stance is the difference between the fairy tale and the children's novel. Instead of the abstract, indefinite time of the first novel, the second places the adventures in a specific time setting: 1839. Instead of formulaic presentation of plot and brief characterization through one or two dominant traits in the first, the second includes intricacies of motive and fully developed characters.[13] What Schlegelmilch does not note and what is most significant is that the language changes. In the first novel Lofting depended on language that recalls the diction of folklore, consistently choosing the concrete over the abstract and using transitional words that suggest an oral reteller:

> Then John Dolittle got a fine, big pair of green spectacles . . .
> And soon it became a common sight . . .
> And so it was . . .
> Now all these animals went back and told . . . (14–15)

These openings, drawn from four successive paragraphs in *The Story of Doctor Dolittle,* recall the links used in verbal retellings and lend a sense of folklore to the story. None of this appears in *The Voyages of Doctor Dolittle,* for it is no longer a "story" but a recounting by a specific narrator of a specific time.

The most important difference between the two novels is this narrator. "My name was Tommy Stubbins, son of Jacob Stubbins, the cobbler of Puddleby-on-the-Marsh; and I was nine years old"[14] begins *The Voyages of Doctor Dolittle.* Despite the prominence of the Doctor's name in the title, the character who is most significant in terms of the craft of the tale and the reader's response is not the Doctor but Tommy Stubbins, son of Jacob Stubbins the cobbler and Doctor Dolittle's fellow voyager. Stubbins is Lofting's finest and most subtly crafted creation, one of the few Lofting characters who undergo recognizable development and change, and the major vehicle for meaning and interpretation in the second novel.

Stubbins's role as narrator is marked by his acute sensibility, for in all the novels his is the only character whose sensibility is close to that of the reader. Because of his unchanging nature and absorbing interests, the Doctor remains a bit remote, and the reader never sees things entirely from his perspective alone; he is always being created and interpreted for the reader. Dolittle becomes central for the reader only because he is central to Stub-

bins. And so Stubbins, the practical, dependable lad with somewhat limited perspectives but an inordinate desire to journey and
to adventure, becomes the reader's vicarious adventurer. He in-
terprets and understands the way the reader would interpret and
understand. He moves and has his being in the world of the novels in the same way that the reader would move and have being
if suddenly, mysteriously, the reader were transported to the seawall overlooking Puddleby-on-the-Marsh.

The prologue of *The Voyages of Doctor Dolittle* is enormously
important in terms of the meaning of what is to come and the role
of the narrator in conveying that meaning. Stubbins begins without announcing his name; that is to come in the opening chapter.
Yet he instantly establishes rather significant links with the first
novel of the series, *The Story of Doctor Dolittle*. "All that I have
written so far about Doctor Dolittle," Stubbins writes, "I heard
long after it happened from those who had known him—indeed,
a great deal of it took place before I was born. But now I come to
set down that part of the great man's life which I myself saw and
took part in" (1). This passage represents a dramatic change in
stance, for Lofting here announces his intention to move from the
omniscient narrator of *The Story of Doctor Dolittle* to the first-
person-limited narrator, a change that invigorates several of the
other novels in the series.

It is also a move that shifts the focus of attention, for the first
three chapters deal almost exclusively with Stubbins. And even
when the Doctor is introduced as the two characters collide in a
rainstorm, the reader's focus remains on Stubbins, for the reader
can see only what Stubbins sees. The reader watches with Stubbins as Dab-Dab, holding the lighted candle, comes down the
stairs; the reader shares his astonishment. With Stubbins the
reader sees Doctor Dolittle plunge his head into a tank of water
to learn the language of the Wiff-Waff; the reader shares Stubbins's incredulity. And even the voyages that Dolittle and Stubbins undertake together come about in principle because of
Stubbins's yearning to follow the mast of the tall ships down the
Puddleby River and out to unknown faerie seas.

"*I would sit on the river-wall with my feet dangling over the water.*"

29

This passage has another implication most critics have ignored: Stubbins himself claims that he is the narrator of *The Story of Doctor Dolittle*. There are a number of difficulties with this claim. Perhaps the least important of these is that Lofting gives no indication that he had conceived of the character of Stubbins during the writing of the first novel; indeed, the way in which the tales were developed would suggest that he did not, for none of the letters sent home from the fronts of World War I in which he first worked out these stories mention Stubbins.

But an even more important difference—one Schlegelmilch does not consider—lies in the eye of the narrator. The description of the first novel is rather sparse; Lofting limits it to only that which is absolutely essential to the development of the plot itself. Even those settings which would seem to be exotic and interesting in themselves, as well as those which might play some thematic role, are only sketchily drawn. But the narrator of the second novel has quite a different eye. In the opening chapter Stubbins, the nine-and-a-half-year-old boy, sits on the river wall, dangles his feet over the water, and muses about his trips out to the edge of the sea with Joe, the mussel man:

> And out there on the cold lonely marshes we would see wild geese flying, and curlews and redshanks and many other kinds of seabirds that live among the samfire and the long grass of the great salt fen. And as we crept up the river in the evening, when the tide had turned, we would see the light on Kingsbridge twinkle in the dusk, reminding us of tea-time and warm fires. (4)

The very structure of the passage, with its opening conjunctions linking idea and image with idea and image, suggests a completely different approach to the telling of the tale from that of the narrator of *The Story of Doctor Dolittle*. Images themselves convey both literal and metaphoric meaning. The seabirds fly above him and call him out to the ocean, but he is also called to the domestic security of tea and warm fires so important to a young child. There are no similar constructions and no similar evocations of imagery in the first novel.

This descriptive passage quite obviously does not come from the sensibility of a nine-year-old. Instead, it grows out of a second major implication of the prologue to *The Voyages of Doctor Dolittle*: the Stubbins who is writing is now an old man. "Many years ago," he narrates, "the Doctor gave me permission [to write of our adventures]. . . . Now of course, when I am quite an old man, my memory isn't so good any more. But whenever I am in doubt and have to hesitate and think, I always ask Polynesia, the parrot" (1). The perspective is that of a man remembering his own past and recalling the events that have shaped his life. This is a recollection in tranquillity, where he is able to look back and order and shape the events into a rather tidy progression. This perspective accounts for the numerous moments when the narrator steps back from the progress of the plot to muse about the meaning of the action or his memory of it. When Stubbins comes to relate the attacks of the Bag-jagderags on Spidermonkey Island, he pauses in the midst of a series of short paragraphs dealing exclusively with the action to establish a sense of distance between himself and the events of that day. "I now come to a part in the story of our voyages," he writes, "where things happened so quickly, one upon the other, that looking backwards I see the picture only in a confused sort of way" (278). That self-conscious analysis of his narration suggests Lofting's concern with establishing the credibility of this narrator and with linking that narrator to the reader's own perceptions.

This perspective also links the two novels. Both books begin with some attempt to establish the action in terms of time; the first opens with a purposefully vague reference to time, employing a formulaic opening that begins all the really great stories of the world: "Once upon a time, many years ago—when our grandfathers were little children—there was a doctor; and his name was Dolittle—John Dolittle, M.D." (1). Leaving aside the fact that this leads to some difficulties in terms of Stubbins's claim that he is the narrator of the first novel, the opening brings us—espe-

cially the child reader—back into a time that is remote because
it is beyond our memory.

The second novel is similarly remote, and the time frame is
established through relating the events to characters and setting
within the context of the story. After announcing that he was nine
and a half, Stubbins writes, "At that time Puddleby was only
quite a small town. A river ran through the middle of it; and over
this river there was a very old stone bridge, called Kingsbridge,
which led you from the market-place on one side to the church-
yard on the other" (3). Here Lofting, through Stubbins, evokes a
time frame that is remote in terms of the personal histories of the
characters. Stubbins recalls Puddleby-on-the-Marsh as it once
must have been and is, presumably, no longer. But despite this
difference, both novels open with a similar concern: the desire to
put the action of the story beyond the reader's memory and
experience.

The action of the story seems to begin where *The Story of Doctor Dolittle* leaves off. *The Voyages of Doctor Dolittle* begins with
a self-assured, confident, though still unassuming Dolittle. He is
pictured as a frequent traveler; in fact, the narrator notes that
Dolittle took voyages even prior to the days when Sarah left
him—this in contradiction to the first novel. But the early emphasis on travel is significant, for Dolittle's inclination to voyage
is the organizing focus of this otherwise somewhat disjointed,
rambling novel.

The book begins with Tommy's introduction of himself and his
yearning to travel to distant ports. He also has an inclination to
be a naturalist, and when he finds a squirrel with a broken leg
he brings it home and tries his best to mend it. On the advice of
Matthew Mugg, Tommy tries to seek the counsel of Doctor Dolittle, who is on a voyage. After frequent visits to the Doctor's house,
Tommy accidentally meets him on a rainy day as they collide in
the street. The Doctor brings Tommy into his house, treats him
like an adult (he refers to him as Stubbins), and introduces him
to his animal household. Tommy soon becomes accepted as a
member of the family, and he begins to learn animal language as
the Doctor tries to learn the language of shellfish. The Doctor

eventually visits Tommy's parents, and Tommy is apprenticed as a naturalist. The boy is particularly delighted, since this ensures that he will sail on the Doctor's next voyage.

When the time comes to travel, the Doctor seeks out a third human crew member: Luke the Hermit. When he finds him, however, Luke has been arrested on an old murder charge; only Luke's dog can tell the truth of what happened. During the trial the Doctor convinces the judge that he can indeed speak to animals. Once the truth comes out, Luke is freed and reunited with his wife. Thus he is lost as a potential crew member, but the position is filled by Prince Bumpo, a character from *The Story of Doctor Dolittle,* who principally serves as comic relief for the reader. "You are a man of great studiosity," he tells the Doctor. "To see the world in your company is an opportunity not to be sneezed upon. No, no, indeed" (150).

The destination of the voyage is determined by chance. Dolittle had wished to meet Long Arrow, another great naturalist, but when Miranda, the purple bird of paradise, flies from the Southern Hemisphere to tell Dolittle that Long Arrow is missing, Dolittle decides to open his atlas and let Stubbins choose a place with his eyes closed. He chooses Spidermonkey Island, a curious choice for two reasons: it is a floating island and it is the last known location of Long Arrow.

The ship is loaded and, to the cheering of the townsfolk, Dolittle and company set out on the voyage. They are hindered from heading straight to Spidermonkey Island, however. They are momentarily trapped on a sandbar. They stop to put off Matthew, who had wished to travel with the Doctor, and another sailor, who had determined that the Doctor, to survive, needed him. They put to port in Monteverde for supplies, and there the Doctor ends the practice of bullfighting by putting on a spectacular show with three bulls that shames the other bullfighters. They capture a small fish, a fidgit, who tells his story of being caught in an English aquarium while the ship drifts with no one to steer. Eventually the ship is wrecked in a storm, and the crew is saved by a school of porpoises that push the wrecked hulk to Spidermonkey Island.

Once there, Dolittle finds a rare beetle that carries a message from Long Arrow: he and several others are trapped in a cave. Using the beetle as a guide, Dolittle locates the cave and frees Long Arrow, and the two great naturalists meet for the first time. This feat ensures the Doctor's acceptance by the other natives of Spidermonkey Island, as Long Arrow introduces him to the Popsipetel tribe. The Doctor brings fire to the village and helps defend the village in a battle against the island's other tribe, the Bag-jagderags. Here they are helped by thousands of black parrots summoned by Polynesia, and the two tribes force Dolittle to become king over both of them, a position that seems to end Dolittle's chance of studying shellfish languages. As king, Dolittle calls on a school of whales to move the island back to its proper position (it had been blown too far south by the same storm that wrecked the Doctor's ship), and brings English customs to the island. He also presides at a coronation during which the island sinks a bit and is joined to the ocean floor.

A year goes by, and the Doctor is completely dominated by his duties as king. When the Great Sea Snail appears from the island's coast, Tommy, Bumpo, and Polynesia and the other animals see this as a chance for Dolittle to escape. Much against his will, they convince him to leave, and they all clamber into the snail's shell for a voyage beneath the ocean to their home in England. (Though the snail is not pictured in the published edition, Lofting did draw an illustration of the creature, later published in a 1967 collection.) On the way, the Doctor keeps copious notes and does eventually learn shellfish language. On arriving at the English coast, they conclude that "there's something rather attractive in the bad weather of England—when you've got a kitchen fire to look forward to" (364).

This convoluted, episodic plot finds its unity in the narrator. Stubbins is the selective lens through which we see Doctor Dolittle; our perspective and our knowledge are consistently dependent on his own. And that perspective is not that of a naturalist. It is instead that of a writer, of one who is consciously telling a tale and who sees this telling as the most important part of his endeavor.

When Stubbins is first introduced, he almost seems a character out of the opening chapter of a Robert Louis Stevenson novel. Because his father is poor, he does not go to school but instead spends his time dealing with the natural world, collecting blackberies and mushrooms and birds' eggs. But—and here is his most important trait in terms of these novels—he yearns to escape the narrow boundaries of Puddleby-on-the-Marsh. "Like all boys," he muses, "I wanted to grow up—not knowing how well off I was with no cares and nothing to worry me. Always I longed for the time when I should be allowed to leave my father's house, to take passage in one of those brave ships, to sail down the river through the misty marshes to the sea—out into the world to seek my fortune" (7). This passage shows an almost unutterable longing for that which is other, for that which is beyond the marshy limits. The repeating parallel clauses—typical of Stubbins's style—suggest the intensity of his yearning.

In the very next chapter Polynesia, motivated by her desire to find an assistant for the Doctor and by Stubbins's yearning to know more of the man, introduces Stubbins to the language of the animals. And once the forms of the apprenticeship are established and Stubbins's parents have agreed, the boy is happy not so much about becoming a naturalist as about something quite different.

> At last the dream of my life was to come true! At last I was to be given a chance to seek my fortune, to have adventures! . . . Polynesia had told me that he hardly ever stayed at home for more than six months at a stretch. Therefore, he would be surely going again within a fortnight. And I—I, Tommy Stubbins, would go with him! Just to think of it!—to cross the Sea, to walk on foreign shores, to roam the World! (87)

His joy is a boyish one—at the thought of the journey itself. Here is his chance to achieve all he had so ardently wished for on the river-wall by Puddleby-on-the-Marsh. (He has not yet come to realize that he has already found his fortune.) But the boyish excitement is expressed from the perspective of an older narrator remembering that excitement, for his expression of disordered and chaotic emotion is set in a very ordered way. The first two sentences open with the matching phrase "at last," suggesting a sense of released frustration and expected fulfillment. Two sentences of quick analysis follow, and then the writing seems to stutter in Stubbins's excitement: "And I—I, Tommy Stubbins." The section is concluded with three parallel infinitive clauses whose balance suggests emotion recollected and ordered in tranquillity.

For children, much of the pleasure of the novels may lie in this story of Tommy Stubbins. During the action of the tales, he is the character who is closest in terms of the experience of the child, and many of his dreams and desires mirror the dreams and desires of all children: to be loved, to be respected as an individual, to learn, to adventure. These are needs all children recognize, and in the rather strange and foreign worlds of Doctor Dolittle they seem remarkably familiar. Stubbins's growth is that of a child to an adult, as the reader participates in it over the course of the Doctor Dolittle series.

That growth comes about as two latent tendencies in Stubbins—his desire to travel and his yearning to be a naturalist—are developed during the apprenticeship to Dolittle. Their first meeting reveals a mutual recognition of these traits, as Stubbins is welcomed into the Doctor's household by the Doctor himself and his extraordinary animal family. Yet what initially attracts Stubbins to the Doctor is not his ability to speak animal languages but the Doctor's respect for him. Just before they meet, Stubbins has two unpleasant experiences with the adult world in the form of Colonel Bellows, who sees in the boy a somewhat irritating wretch who does not know his place as a child and servant. Dolittle, on the other hand, brings him into his house, dries his clothes made wet by a sudden storm, asks him to stay for dinner, and discusses his work as a naturalist on a serious level. Stubbins's reaction is predictable.

> Already I was beginning to be very fond of this funny
> little man who called me "Stubbins," instead of "Tommy"
> or "little lad" (I did so hate being called "little lad"!). This

man seemed to begin right away treating me as though
I were a grownup friend of his. And when he asked me
to stop and have supper with him I felt terribly proud
and happy. (25)

Perhaps because of this sense of respect from someone whom he
recognizes as a rather important man, Stubbins expresses only a
little strangeness at the situation in which he finds himself: a
house filled with animals who are speaking to the Doctor and
carrying out household chores. He mentions no sense of oddity
when the Doctor comes to his house and speaks to the lame squirrel Stubbins has been tending, or when the Doctor promises to
send another squirrel to bring him news of his family. A kinship
is already developing between two characters who both long for
voyages and who both care for animals.

The morning after this initial visit, Stubbins returns to the
Doctor's house; the gate that was formerly closed to him because
of the Doctor's absence is now open. Jip is no longer there to keep
him out, and instead he is cheerfully greeted by Polynesia, who
complains about England's beastly weather and then says, "Well,
don't let me keep you. Run along and see the Doctor" (46). From
that moment on, Stubbins is recognized as a part of the household. When he finds the Doctor he is greeted in one sentence, and
two sentences later he is drawn into the work of the great naturalist. After this he is a part of not only the household but the
doctor's work.

The remainder of *The Voyages of Doctor Dolittle* chronicles the
voyage that Stubbins is so eager to go on, and it is, for the most
part, one that is completely different from the other voyages the
doctor takes. Their destination is motivated by pure chance,
rather than by design. This is not really an expedition of discovery, and perhaps as a result very little scientific activity goes on,
particularly in comparison to the other books. Stubbins is an active participant in the adventures of the novel, thus fulfilling his
desire for such adventures, but there is as yet no real indication
here that he will become a naturalist himself. That will come in
the succeeding books.

Dolittle, in taking on a mentor role, leaves behind some of the characteristics that shape his childlikeness in *The Story of Doctor Dolittle*. The sense of irresponsibility is gone, as is a certain naïveté about the world. He deals with Stubbins's parents on an adult level, not as a child-cum-adult. He is also pictured as a serious naturalist, something not indicated in the earlier work. Now certainly some of this comes about because Dolittle is being viewed from a child's perspective, but that had been true of the first novel as well, though the perspective was less overt. The suggestion here, if one can link the two novels, is that the act of mentoring itself changes Dolittle. He is not, as the Dolittle series sometimes seems to suggest, as changeless as an Egyptian pyramid.

Stubbins himself does not take on the childlike qualities that Dolittle abandons; at least, an older narrator looking back does not ascribe those qualities to a young self. Instead, Stubbins emphasizes Dolittle's growing involvement in some of the concerns mentioned in *The Story of Doctor Dolittle*. Once again there is the Doctor's concern for humane treatment of both the animal and the human worlds. He clears Luke the Hermit of an unjust murder charge, eliminates bullfighting in Monteverde, frees Long Arrow, saves the tribes of Spidermonkey Island from extinction by war and by a changing climate, and transforms a culture to ensure justice and peace. And to accomplish those goals, Dolittle becomes responsible in ways that the Dolittle of the first novel would not recognize. About to be crowned king of the Popsipetels, Dolittle laments:

> "Oh I know it sounds grand," said he, pulling on his boots miserably. 'But the trouble is, you can't take up responsibilities and then just drop them again when you feel like it. I have my own work to do. Scarcely one moment have I had to give to natural history since I landed on this island. I've been doing some one else's business all the time. And now they want me to go on doing it! Why, once I'm made King of the Popsipetels, that's the end of me as a useful naturalist. I'd be too busy for anything. All I'd be then is just a er—er—just a king." (302)

Nevertheless, he does take on the role, leaving it only when his responsibilities as a naturalist become more important.

The other concern that Stubbins focuses is that of recording story. Dolittle himself indicates—for the first time in the series—an interest that would dominate several of the later novels: an interest in the history of the world. In the beginning of *The Voyages of Doctor Dolittle,* the Doctor indicates his desire to learn the language of shellfish: "We find their shells in the rocks—turned to stone—thousands of years old. So I feel quite sure that if I could only get to talk their language, I should be able to learn a whole lot about what the world was like ages and ages and ages ago" (24). In fact, though he would not learn much from this source, this interest would continue into *Doctor Dolittle in the Moon* and *Doctor Dolittle and the Secret Lake.* The concern for this history is not important only as a curiosity. History would, for Dolittle, become a way of moving back in time to a less cruel age, to a time dominated by gentleness and understanding. His interest extends before man's dominance and explores the very origins of animal life.

And herein lies the death throes of the Edenic worlds of the Victorian and Edwardian children's authors. In Kenneth Grahame's arcadian world the rushes might part and one might look "in the very eyes of the Friend and Helper," and see "the long supple hand still holding the pan-pipes only just fallen away from the parted lips."[15] In Frances Hodgson Burnett's secret garden one might, at any moment, hear golden trumpets or the doxology, "and if all the flowers and leaves and green things and birds and wild creatures danced past at once, what a crowd it would be!"[16] A. A. Milne's Hundred-Akre Wood is a place where "a little boy and his Bear will always be playing,"[17] not unlike the Neverland of J. M. Barrie. Each of these gardens is a place of rest, of rejuvenation, of renewed youth. Each invites its innocents in to be refreshed and to exercise the imagination.

Dolittle too has a garden, walled severely against the outside world. It too is a secret garden, but it is also exclusive; aside from Stubbins, Dolittle, and the animal family, no one—certainly no human being—enters the garden. It is a place of refuge as well as

rest, refuge from a world quite different from the gentle community of Dolittle's household. It is a refuge especially for the animals, who see it as an escape from the burdens imposed on them
by humanity. At the end of the first novel, Dolittle himself falls
asleep in the garden, clutching a scientific book about the dog,
apparently recovering from the adventures in Africa and England. This marks the only time in the novel when the doctor
seems to be at rest.

Stubbins himself is first attracted to the house because of the
garden, and he finds in it a true Eden:

> It had everything—everything a garden can have, or
> ever has had. There were wide, wide lawns with carved
> stone seats, green with moss. Over the lawns hung weep-
> ing-willow, and their feathery bough-tips brushed the
> velvet grass when they swung with the wind. The old
> flagged paths had high, clipped, yew hedges either side
> of them, so that they looked like the narrow streets of
> some old town; and through the hedges, doorways had
> been made; and over the doorways were shapes like
> vases and peacocks and half-moons all trimmed out of
> the living trees. There was a lovely marble fishpond with
> golden carp and blue water-lilies in it and big green
> frogs. A high brick wall alongside the kitchen garden was
> all covered with pink and yellow peaches ripening in the
> sun. There was a wonderful great oak, hollow in the
> trunk, big enough for four men to hide inside. Many sum-
> mer-houses there were, too—some of wood and some of
> stone; and one of them was full of books to read. In a
> corner, among some rocks and ferns, was an outdoor fire-
> place, where the Doctor used to fry liver and bacon when
> he had a notion to take his meals in the open air. There
> was a couch as well on which he used to sleep, it seems,
> on warm summer nights when the nightingales were
> singing at their best; it had wheels on it so it could be
> moved about under any tree they sang in. But the thing
> that fascinated me most of all was a tiny little treehouse,

high up in the top branches of a great elm, with a long rope ladder leading to it. The doctor told me he used it for looking at the moon and the stars through a telescope.

It was the kind of a garden where you could wander and explore for days and days—always coming upon something new, always glad to find the old spots over again. That first time that I saw the Doctor's garden I was so charmed by it that I felt I would like to live in it— always and always and never go outside of it again. For it had everything within its walls to give happiness, to make living pleasant—to keep the heart at peace. It was the Garden of Dreams. (55–57)

Stubbins's description evokes an untainted world, and indeed he later notes that animals that would have been natural enemies outside of the garden here live in harmony. Physically, the garden is a perfect combination of art and nature. Like Elizabeth Bennett approaching Pemberley, Stubbins "had never seen a place for which nature had done more, or where natural beauty had been so little counteracted by an awkward taste."[18]

Stubbins finds here a place "to give happiness, to make life pleasant—to keep the heart at peace." It is a place that Rat and Mole and Colin and Dickon and Christopher Robin and Peter Pan and Wendy would all have recognized, for it is a product of the golden age of Victorian children's literature. But—and here is the point of departure—despite its attraction, neither Stubbins nor Dolittle is content to remain there. Stubbins is wrong: the garden cannot keep the heart at peace. The Doctor cannot rest in his house more than several months; Stubbins is in transports of ec- stasy when he learns he is about to voyage to Spidermonkey Is- land. Both are restless, eager to leave the so-called Garden of Dreams. It is as if Eden is a bore.

In *Secret Gardens* Humphrey Carpenter groups Lofting with Victorian and Edwardian children's writers who pictured En- gland as rural paradise, and complains that Lofting added noth- ing new and distinctive to that tradition.[19] But Lofting is not part of that tradition; he is a repudiator of it. Lofting's characters do not search for Eden; they have left it behind. This has come about not because of the notion that they have matured out of the need for paradise but because paradise—a place to keep the heart at peace—is not really possible. It is a Garden of Dreams, but it is that only.

The result is that, in Lofting's work, the Victorian garden is no longer a real goal; it is a starting place. Dolittle's adventures begin there and move rapidly away; it is never an end in itself. If Lofting is not a member of Gertrude Stein's generation, he is still not willing to create a character who is whole and secure in an Eden. And, in fact, even the security that that character does have will be undermined as the series progresses. For Dolittle— and for Lofting—there is something more important to be done than simply reclining in Eden.

For Lofting, writing after the horror of a world at war with itself, it could not be otherwise.

3

The Dolittle Series:
Variations on Theme and Structure

In *The Voyages of Doctor Dolittle* Lofting had, it seemed, found a structure on which he could play multiple variations. A single motif—a voyage to Africa, a circus, a post office, a secret lake, a green canary—could become the central focus around which tales would spin off. That the tales radiating away from the center were unrelated was not, to Lofting, especially problematic; as long as the central motif was well established, the structure of the book would hold together. Certainly the technique had worked in *The Voyages of Doctor Dolittle,* and early reviewers found little to criticize in the later novels. Nevertheless, the history of the next five novels in the Dolittle series is a history of the gradual decline in inventiveness and the eventual breakdown in the pattern.

Olga Fricker recalls that Lofting believed short stories were more agreeable to children than longer novels, and so his novels were actually conceived as a series of short tales.[1] The result is a kind of built-in disunity and discontinuity; none of the later novels would work toward the inevitable and comic and gentle conclusions of the first two novels. This process has itself led to discontinuity in critical responses to these middle books in the Dolittle series. Margaret Blount, for example, argues that the later novels "tend to be lengthy and tedious, with dull spaces between incidents which have almost the perfection of the original, but are not built up with the original logical crescendo."[2] In contrast, Roger Lancelyn Green suggests that although Lofting never equaled the fantasy of *The Story of Doctor Dolittle,* the later novels are "far more exciting as adventure stories," though he never defines the distinction between the two genres.[3] For Edward Blishen, the books between *Doctor Dolittle's Post Office* and *Doctor Dolittle's Caravan* "form the ebullient, happy center of the series. . . . [T]hey bear all the marks of Lofting's headlong delight in his own invention and in the world of fantastic creation to which it gave him entrance."[4]

The choice of "headlong" is particularly felicitous, for the next five books would be written at the pace of one each year. They would begin in comedy and merriment, filled with an abundance of delightful comic detail. They would end with a different Dolittle, one more serious, more morally centered on the affairs of humanity, more, as it were, affected by a terrible war.

Doctor Dolittle's Post Office

In 1923, following a Newbery Medal, Lofting published *Doctor Dolittle's Post Office.* A large miscellany of stories, its center is a bird-run postal system that Dolittle establishes on the coast of West Africa. The adventures that engage Dolittle are all initiated by the creatures of the post office or by letters from animals that come into it. Some of these adventures have almost nothing to do with Dolittle; he is the silent magnet for tales, thus beginning a technique that Lofting would use more and more frequently until its full fruition in *Doctor Dolittle and the Secret Lake.* In that later novel Dolittle is neither an initiator nor a major actor in the plot; he is a catalyst or a mediator who establishes the situation within which the story will be told. In *Doctor Dolittle's Post Office* that process is just beginning.

The narrator of *Doctor Dolittle's Post Office* is important as one considers the narrative voices of the later novels. In this third novel Lofting made a mistake that he rectified in the later novels:

the central motif—here the post office—is not enough to give unity to a novel filled with disparate stories. Nor is Dolittle himself enough, particularly since he is not prominent in many of the stories. Lofting had solved the problem of unity in *The Voyages of Doctor Dolittle* by using the strong narrative voice of Tommy Stubbins. Curiously, here Stubbins is absent. The result is that there is no strong voice establishing a context for the episodes and a way of understanding their significance; nor is there any voice bridging the distance between the reader and the character of Dolittle. Lofting would learn from the mistake when he came to write *Doctor Dolittle's Zoo*.

But early reviewers did not, apparently, notice the difficulties that were entering the series. Instead, they centered on the character of the Doctor himself as the point of principal focus. "Even a three-year acquaintance with Dr. Dolittle cannot take away from his original, whimsical self a trace of that which endeared him to us. Through his mail service, as through his voyages, he remains always the inimitable Dr. Dolittle," Constance Naar declared in her review for the *New Republic*.[5] The reviewer for the *New York Times Book Review* seemed eager to establish the *Dolittle* books as part of the canon of children's literature classics:

> This third volume of the doings of Doctor Dolittle carries on the activities of that most delightful and entertaining gentleman in the same manner which won instant recognition for Mr. Lofting's preceding stories as children's classics. In this new one the busy and resourceful doctor establishes a Post Office and happily and successfully combines the practice of medicine with the duties of being a Postmaster.... Hugh Lofting's mind dances along, as it did in the other stories about Doctor Dolittle, with the greatest ease and agility from one delicious fantasy to another.... This new book makes secure his seat among the best writers for children of all time.[6]

That the novel actually began the decline in the Dolittle series that would not be arrested until *Doctor Dolittle in the Moon* is no small irony. But it is the focus of these reviews that is most tell-ing. Only a handful of years past a world war, writing about a series spawned by a war experience, the reviewers found a char-acter who was as imperturbable, as selfless, as heroic, and as staunch as anyone could be in the face of even the most dreadful of circumstances. The adjectives the reviewers apply to this char-acter—*original, whimsical, inimitable, busy, resourceful, delight-ful*—are adjectives that might as well have been applied to the ideal country gentlemen of prewar Britain. And here he was still, on the far side of the war, and he had not changed. Thus can children's literature become, for some adult readers, an adventure in nostalgia.

But the reviewer for the *New York Times Book Review* also noted another element in *Doctor Dolittle's Post Office* beyond the character of Doctor Dolittle: the brisk movement between plot ep-isodes—a quality that would mark many of the forthcoming Do-little books. *Doctor Dolittle's Post Office* is actually a recounting of one of the many voyages to which Stubbins refers at the begin-ning of *The Voyages of Doctor Dolittle*; in chronological time these adventures occur between the time of *The Story of Doctor Dolittle* and that of *The Voyages of Doctor Dolittle*. The novel itself begins as Dolittle is heading home from a West African voyage: "One morning in the first week of the return voyage when John Dolittle and his animals were all sitting at breakfast round the big table in the cabin, one of the swallows came down and said that he wanted to speak to the Doctor."[7] This somewhat abrupt but en-grossing opening—the reader is immediately drawn into the ac-tion—presupposes a knowledge of Dolittle, of his animal family, and of his facility with animal languages. Lofting supplies none of this. And this, of course, is the very stuff of a series, where a reader comes to a novel armed with some knowledge and as-sumptions about the characters, settings, and plot situations.

The swallow has come to report a canoe drifting aimlessly in the ocean, and Dolittle at once sets out to the rescue. He discovers Zuzana, who had set off in pursuit of the slavers who had taken her husband. Aided by a British warship and thousands of spar-rows, Dolittle does indeed effect the rescue and finds that Zuzana's husband had been taken because of a delay in the postal system. Dolittle resolves to begin a new, more efficient system—though, the narrator warns, "little did he realize what great labors and strange adventures he was taking upon himself" (40).

Dolittle eventually establishes his post office in a houseboat floating off the shore of Fantippo, by an island that has become a kind of Eden for animals; no human being goes there, fearful of the supposed dragons. There Dolittle meets with thousands of birds and establishes the mail system by working with the birds' migration habits and routes. The system is meant to serve both humanity and the animal kingdom. Cheapside, the Cockney London sparrow, is brought in to organize the domestic mail, and soon all is in readiness.

From this beginning Dolittle does indeed encounter strange adventures. He meets a jay who tells the story of how his ancestors saved Christopher Columbus and led that mariner to the New World. Dolittle saves a ship from running aground when he, with the help of some gulls, relights the Cape Stephen Lighthouse. The postal system yields the side benefits of initiating a weather bureau, a series of animal correspondence courses, and an animal journal. Interest in the journal is encouraged by the publication of a series of stories by the Doctor's animal family, each of whom tells an episode from his or her own life.

Dolittle eventually establishes a parcel post so that such things as bicycles can be shipped to Fantippo. But this leads to a robbery, as two pearls are apparently stolen. When a squirrel returns them, Dolittle himself travels to the village of Chief Nyam-Nyam, whose lands are constantly being taken over by other tribes and whose people are becoming impoverished. Dolittle routs a band of attacking Amazons with the help of hordes of white mice and asks a cormorant to fish up pearl oysters; soon the village is wealthy. When Dolittle is imprisoned by a neighboring king who aspires to the wealth of the pearls, he is saved by his animal family in such a way as to make the natives think he has great magical powers.

Returning to the post office, Dolittle receives two letters from Mudface the turtle, offering to recite for Dolittle his eyewitness account of Noah's flood. Dolittle travels through mangrove swamps to the Secret Lake of Junganyika, where he spends several days listening to the turtle's story (a story that is not to be given to the reader until the publication of *Doctor Dolittle and the Secret Lake*). When he returns to Fantippo, he realizes that it is time for him to go back to England. The Fantippons erect a wooden statue and reluctantly bid farewell, though they continue to tend the flower boxes of the post office in hope of Dolittle's return.

The plot is markedly episodic, the post office providing the initial impetus for the adventures. The delight comes in what the *New York Times Book Review* writer calls the movement "from one delicious fantasy to another." These episodes are variations on themes: the animal version of history, the spectacular rescue, the dominance of Dolittle in African society. All of these themes had been played in both prior novels; the success of *Doctor Dolittle's Post Office* is measured by the degree to which Lofting could continue to invent within the confines of these themes.

The nature of the narrator of *Doctor Dolittle's Post Office* is enigmatic. The prologue of the novel suggests that the narrator will be a dominant presence; indeed, the very opening of the prologue, with its emphasis on the "I," the teller of the story, suggests such a presence: "Nearly all of the history of Doctor Dolittle's post office took place when he was returning from a voyage to West Africa. Therefore I will begin (as soon as I have told you a little about how he came to take the journey) from where he turned his ship towards home again and set sail for Puddleby-on-the-Marsh" (1). The voice here—reasoned, level, rather matter-of-fact—seems to be that of Stubbins, but in fact Stubbins is never mentioned. The voice is that of the anonymous storyteller, though once one has read the later books, it seems that this may indeed be Stubbins, recording the adventure as it was later recounted for him. But the context of this novel alone does not allow for that interpretation.

The narrator concludes the prologue with another reference to his part in telling the story—"And it is from this point that my story begins" (2)—but then fades back, so as not to stand between the reader and the Doctor. For the next 300 pages the narrator will retain a detached pose, breaking in overtly only once more, at the beginning of the Mudface incident: "We are now come to an unusual event in the history of the Doctor's post office, to the one which was, perhaps, the greatest of all the curious things that came about through the institution of the Swallow Mail" (310). Here the narrator is using his own fictive responses to mediate the reactions of the reader. Whether or not the reader will think the next incident the most curious, the narrator has established something of his own participatory nature in noting his own response. The narrator too seems involved in the tale; he is not so detached as his tone has seemed to indicate.

And, in fact, though this narrator has neither the insights into Dolittle's character nor the relationship with his animal family that Stubbins has, he is still highly sympathetic, thoroughly caught up in the charm of the tale. Nevertheless, he is not as close as Stubbins to the characters and the adventures, and so his voice is unable to make the kinds of connections between episodes that Stubbins's voice can make; this narrator cannot provide the kind of overall unity that Stubbins will provide, and he cannot make the kinds of assessments that Stubbins can make. Nor can a reader identify with this narrator as well as with Stubbins. The essential lack of unity in *Doctor Dolittle's Post Office* can be traced directly to the detached narrator, who sees episodes as isolated and for the most part independent.

Lofting did develop a technique in *Doctor Dolittle's Post Office* that he would employ again and again: the story-within-a-story. Here Dolittle's presence in the plot situation is a catalyst for a tale he will often act on. On a small scale this technique begins the novel, as Dolittle comes upon Zuzana, who is drifting in a canoe. At first suspicious, she is reluctant to speak with Dolittle; "[l]ittle by little, however, the Doctor won her confidence and at last, still weeping bitterly, she told him her story" (6). Once she finishes telling her story, the narrator completes the tale with Dolittle's reaction: "The Doctor was dreadfully angry when he had heard the story" (7). This is the pattern Lofting uses; its principal advantage is that it establishes plot situations and provides the impetus for Dolittle's actions. Here, Zuzana's story sends Dolittle off after the slavers.

But Lofting's strength is that he is able to use patterns for multiple purposes. At times the framing device is used to bring in a group of tales that are included only for their elements of delight; they bring nothing to the current plot situations except for a kind of leisurely tone. The central portion of the novel is devoted to a story told by Dolittle, followed by stories by Gub-Gub, Dab-Dab, the White Mouse, Jip, Too-Too, and the Pushmi-Pullyu. These mark the most prominent roles for the animal characters in *Doctor Dolittle's Post Office,* but the tales themselves are quite irrelevant to the main action. Besides their intrinsic delight, they serve mostly to establish the kind of relaxed life-style of the Doctor on his houseboat.

The same framing device is used to include within the scope of the larger novel stories that are not explicitly connected to the larger novel but are part of its characterization of Dolittle and part of its delightful play with history. In *Doctor Dolittle's Post Office* this technique is used especially in the retelling of Noah's flood and of Columbus's voyage. The sense here is that human history and animal history intermingle, and that human beings do not have the only—or the only true—perspective on events. Human history does not record the jay's decision to help Columbus; nor does it record Mudface's animosity toward the civilization destroyed by the flood. When Dolittle thinks back on Mudface's story, he notes that "it's a story that nobody else could tell" (354); this is a description for many of the framed histories of the Dolittle novels.

And Dolittle himself helps to create stories that can be told by no one else. When he examines Mudface the turtle and prescribes a drier home, Dolittle has the birds of West Africa build an island in the middle of the lake, using stones from the African coast. The narrator emphasizes that the creation of the island is a story that only Dolittle and the animal world can tell: "But that is why, when many years later some learned geologists visited Lake Junganyika, they said that the seashore gravel on an island there was clear proof that the sea had once flowed through that neighborhood. Which was true—in the days of the Flood. But the Doctor was the only scientist who knew that Mudface's island, and the stones that made it, had quite a different history" (354). What Lofting defines as "a different history" is in fact, from the narrator's point of view and the reader's, a true history, hidden from others because they lack Dolittle's linguistic abilities and, perhaps even more important, because they lack Dolittle's perceptive kindness.

Gentle, sturdy, dependable—Dolittle is all of these. Yet it is his essential kindness that is his principal feature, the characteristic almost always mentioned by early reviewers. Clearly this kindness extends to the animal kingdom; in this novel it establishes the impetus for the central endeavor: the founding of the post office. "You see," explains the Doctor, "my idea is, firstly, a post-office system for the advocation and betterment of the Animal Kingdom, and, secondly, a good foreign mail for the Fantippons" (74). He goes on to suggest that "[w]ith a good post-office system of their own, I feel that the condition of the birds and animals will be greatly bettered" (76). Clearly this is of a piece with the fantasy of the novel, but the goal—that conditions in the animal kingdom will be greatly bettered—is not simply a part of the fantasy. None of the novels can ever be read outside the context of the first: the trenches of the First World War, where horses, unprotected against the green billows of gas that belched across the fields and cascaded into the trenches, died screaming out of burning lungs. The order of Dolittle's priorities in establishing the mail service was no accident; it was part of Lofting's vision of who the Doctor was.

But not only horses died in the trenches, and it is to be noted that the Doctor has in no way rejected humanity; not for him the solution of the disenchanted Gulliver. And so here in this novel begins a trend that will be developed much more fully in the "moon" books: the Doctor's conscious desire to help humanity. The trend is only in its infancy here, coming about as a side benefit of the Swallow Mail, when the Doctor establishes a weather bureau: "'I would like,' said the Doctor, 'to be able to prophesy weather for every part of the world. . . . I could improve the farming and the agriculture of the whole human race. But also, and especially, I want to have a bureau for ocean weather, to help the ships'" (152–53). Given the context of the novel, these are small goals, and the narrator informs the reader three pages later that they are achieved. Later novels will heighten the Doctor's goals, so that he yearns to change the very nature of humanity. This is, in some ways, the principal change the Doctor undergoes in the course of the 12 novels.

Part of this kindness comes out of the Doctor's essential self-lessness, a dominating characteristic. In *The Voyages of Doctor Dolittle* it is seen in his commitment to his role as king of Popsi-petel. In *Doctor Dolittle's Post Office* this characteristic is taken to almost absurd lengths. The Doctor, despite chronic monetary difficulties, refuses to accept the proffered gift of two enormous pearls. When the practical Dab-Dab remonstrates, Dolittle observes that "[t]he baby spoonbills want them. . . . Why should I take them away from them?" (281). Later, when Chief Nyam-Nyam presents Dolittle with an enormous pearl as a gift for Dolittle's bringing prosperity to his country, Dolittle almost unthinkingly sends it off to a farmer of brussel sprouts in Lincoln-shire, "to Dab-Dab's horror" (309). The narrator makes no comment, makes no attempt to enter Dolittle's consciousness. For the Doctor, the act of selfless kindness is absolutely instinctive. It is left to the animal family to find rationalizations: "'Easy comes, easy goes,' murmured Gub-Gub. 'Never mind. I don't suppose it's really such fun being rich. Wealthy people have to behave so unnaturally'" (309).

The Doctor's character could seem almost unworldly, were it not for his ability to be raised to wrath and action. This kind and rotund fellow was known as one of the "Terrible Three" in *The Voyages of Doctor Dolittle,* and in *Doctor Dolittle's Post Office* he is similarly angered. He is "dreadfully angry" (7) when he hears the story of Zuzana, and he himself shoots the cannon that brings the slaver to a standstill. Dolittle's amazing endurance enables him to reach the Cape Stephen Lighthouse to save the oncoming ship. Singlehandedly he attacks Wilkins, the pearl thief, and bests him. Alone he overcomes Obombo's rebellion and withstands the pressure of the Emir of Ellebubu, who wishes to steal the rights to the pearl fisheries. In short, at every turn he is a man of physical action.

The most serious charge to be leveled at the Doctor's kindness is that of racism, a charge leveled against several of the Dolittle books. To the narrator of this novel, that charge would have no meaning. But to the contemporary critic, the easy assumption of Dolittle's dominance in almost all matters poses something of a problem. From Dolittle's perspective, this dominance is not racism but simply another manifestation of his essential kindness: he will transform West African society into an African imitation of England for its own betterment; Dolittle is not able to see—nor perhaps was his author—the ethnocentrism involved in such a position. This ignorance on Dolittle's part does lend to some odd moments. When it seems that Zuzana and the Doctor might not be able to rescue Zuzana's husband, he comforts her by "saying that if he failed he would get her another husband, just as good" (8). One can hardly imagine Dolittle's using such a callous comfort for a similar case set in Britain. Zuzana's response is appropriate: "[S]he didn't seem to care for that idea and went on wailing, 'Alas! Alas!'" (8). Even so, Dolittle's own perspective would define this as an act of kindness.

The Doctor is never the source of overt racism himself, though he does seem to participate in the ethnocentrism of his Victorian contemporaries. At times, derogatory remarks will come from the narrator: "The next morning the Doctor was up early. After a light breakfast (it was impossible to get any other in that poverty-stricken country) he asked Nyam-Nyam the way to the Harmatton Rocks" (275). The offhanded tone of this comment, set in almost as an aside, suggests that the narrator is hardly aware of the tone, yet it distinguishes the narrator from the character of Dolittle, who never makes such asides.

The most overt ethnocentrism comes from Cheapside. Speaking to a gull, Cheapside establishes his belligerent stance and bespeaks an attitude not far beneath the surface of Victorian Britain, the period in which this novel is set: "Don't you get turning up your long nautical nose at England, my lad. What do you call

this 'ere? A climate? Well, I should call it a Turkish bath. In England we like variety in our climate. And we get it. That's why
Englishmen 'ave such 'earty red faces. 'ere the poor creatures turn
black" (152). The Doctor, who is present, completely ignores this
statement. Aside from the ethnocentric joke, the use of "poor creatures" by a swallow is such an unutterable act of linguistic condescension that it almost becomes a parody of itself, and one way
to read Cheapside's character is as a satiric attack on mindless
ethnocentrism. Certainly Cheapside's stance is never lauded.

Still, Dolittle is consistently pictured as the great white hero.
He pats old Chief Nyam-Nyam on the back, promising to rescue
him from Obombo. When he achieves prosperity for Nyam-
Nyam's country, he returns to the village looking "like a conquer-
ing general coming back at the head of an army, so many had
gathered to him on the way" (306). He succeeds at establishing a
post office where Koko, the king of Fantippo, had failed. And he
is remembered by the people of Nyam-Nyam "as the greatest man
who had ever visited their land" (306). Here truly is the embodi-
ment of the honest, robust, gentle Victorian gentleman who had
heeded Kipling and gone to take up his proper burden.

Much of the ethnocentrism that comes up in this and subsequent novels is a result of the distinctions Lofting makes between
civilization and noncivilization, or, put more succinctly, between
England and Africa. In establishing a postal system, Dolittle is
transforming an African system into an English system. Cheapside is brought in to advise, and soon the doors are fitted with
brass door knockers and letter slots. The holiday of Christmas is
introduced so that the postal birds will get treats, despite the
meaninglessness of the holiday in that culture. The city is divided
into districts, on the model of London. In short, it is an English
system that is created, right down to the flower boxes on the post
office windows and the gracious afternoon teas on the houseboat.

Yet Lofting is not attempting to set up serious distinctions between England and West Africa; this is still a fantasy novel aimed
at a child audience. And so the distinctions Lofting makes are
ones set in terms that a child—or one of the members of Dolittle's
animal family—would readily understand: the heat of the cli-

mate, the bright door knockers, the flowers on a houseboat, the pastries at afternoon teas. All of these are very sensual elements that a child reader would readily affirm.

Doctor Dolittle's Post Office is remarkable, then, not so much for itself as for its introduction of structural trends and thematic concepts Lofting would develop in the later novels of the series. Those who have dismissed the later books as plodding and predictable have missed the increasingly intricate variations Lofting plays with those trends and themes. But there is one more element Lofting develops in this novel, an element that has both structural and thematic importance: the secret garden.

Humphrey Carpenter, writing of the secret gardens of the Victorian and early Edwardian children's writers, describes such places as arcadias where the child is continually reborn as a child.[8] Secret gardens are secret because they are free from the interference—the corruption, if you will—of the adult world. These are the Neverlands, the enchanted 100-Akre Wood, the willow-lined rivers of Rat and Mole that never change, that securely and continually turn the child world back into itself.

But Lofting's Dolittle, who is so Victorian in so many ways, uses secret gardens quite differently. For Dolittle, they are not the escape but the very center of a search, at least in *Doctor Dolittle's Post Office*. The island off Fantippo known as the animal paradise and the Secret Lake of Junganyika are both secret gardens, not in the sense that they are arcadias—the Secret Lake is surrounded by mangrove swamps and is described as damp and unhealthy—but because they exist apart from human interference. Here animals live out their lives unhindered:

> Down by the banks of the streams the Doctor was shown great herds of hippopotami, feeding on the luscious reeds that grew out of the water's edge. In the wide fields of high grass there were elephants and rhinoceri browsing. On the slopes where the forests were sparse he spied long-necked giraffes, nibbling from the trees. Monkeys and deer of all kinds were plentiful. And birds swarmed everywhere. In fact, every kind of creature that does not

eat meat was there, living peaceably and happily with
the others in this land where vegetable food abounded
and the disturbing tread of Man was never heard (67).

The secret garden here—a kind of wild mirror of Dolittle's own
garden back in Puddleby-on-the-Marsh—is not so much an escape
for Dolittle as an Edenic vision of what life without humanity's
touch is like. Although at this point in the *Dolittle* series this vision is an ideal, later novels will chronicle Dolittle's attempt—and
failure—to make the vision normative.

But in *Doctor Dolittle's Post Office* there is none of the high
seriousness of some of the later novels; it is all a spree. None of
the characters are ever in serious danger; nor is the child reader
manipulated into suspenseful plot situations. Serious overtones
are constantly being subverted. When, for example, Dolittle is
thrown into the prison of the Emir of Ellebubu (the name itself is
a subversion), the narrator works at establishing a tone that negates suspense: "The prison into which the Doctor was thrown
had no windows. And John Dolittle, although he had been in African prisons before, was very unhappy because he was extremely
particular about having fresh air" (293). Later he laments, "What
a poor holiday I am spending, to be sure!" (293). Perhaps this is
the image of the staunch English gentleman, but the effect is to
establish a comic tone in place of a suspenseful one.

And this, of course, is the effect of the illustrations as well. In
the illustration of the prison scene, Dolittle is reclined and at
ease; the emir, erect and straight, is stiff and frustrated and angry (299). Over and over Dolittle is shown at ease, or doing
domestic chores, or as slightly puzzled at the exaggerated posturings of others, as in his reaction to the British sea captain angry
at Dolittle's failure to light the running lights on his ship at night.
Even the illustration of Wilkins leveling a pistol at the Doctor's
head is marked by Dolittle's puzzled expression, his hat set back
from his forehead (262). It seems that he can hardly believe that
someone would pose a real danger for him.

But neither can the child reader. For Dolittle, secure in himself,
is also secure for the child reader. And that element of his character would never change over the course of the 12 novels.

Doctor Dolittle's Circus

Toward the end of *Doctor Dolittle's Post Office,* when the Doctor has been granted a large pearl by the king of Nyam-Nyam, his animal family rejoices:

> "Thank goodness for that!" Dab-Dab whispered to Jip. "Do you realize what that pearl means to us? The Doctor was down to his last shilling—as poor as a church mouse. We would have had to go circus-travelling with the pushmi-pullyu again, if it hadn't been for this. I'm so glad. For, for my part, I shall be glad enough to stay at home and settle down a while—once we get there."
>
> "Oh, I don't know," said Gub-Gub. "I love circuses. I wouldn't mind travelling, so long as it's in England—and with a circus." (307)

When the Doctor gives the pearl away, Jip comments, with a sigh, "Heigh ho! . . . It's a circus for us, all right" (309). And so the motivation for *Doctor Dolittle's Circus* is established. Certainly the later novel can be read without knowledge of the conversation at the pearl fisheries of the Harmatton Rocks, but it is clear that Lofting had conceived of the notion of *Doctor Dolittle's Circus* even before he finished *Doctor Dolittle's Post Office.* Here the circus takes the place of the post office as the novel's central organizing factor, though the circus will be the more potent and evocative of the two.

Doctor Dolittle's Circus tells a tale with a familiar pattern in the Dolittle series. In *The Voyages of Doctor Dolittle* the Doctor becomes king of Popsipetel, and as King Jong he is trapped; he brings such peace and prosperity to the island that he cannot leave. In *Doctor Dolittle's Post Office* he also finds himself trapped; he leaves only after the decision is finally made to discontinue the Swallow Mail. In *Doctor Dolittle's Circus* he becomes, willy-nilly, the manager of Blossom's circus; soon everyone in the circus is dependent on him for his or her survival. And so the familiar pattern emerges: "And now that the Doctor could give the animals the kind of consideration he wished he really enjoyed the life himself a good deal. And poor Dab-Dab began to feel that her chance of getting him away from it, back to his own life at Puddleby, grew dimmer and more distant every day."[9] The opening conjunctions of these two sentences suggest the ongoing nature of this process; for the reader of the series—and certainly for Dab-Dab—this is all familiar, part of the Doctor's character.

The novel begins with the Doctor's recognition that he is in desperate need of funds. He decides to join a circus at which he will exhibit the pushmi-pullyu, who in *The Story of Doctor Dolittle* had agreed to come to England with the Doctor to help him pay for the boat he had lost while in Africa. (By the end of *Doctor Dolittle's Circus* that boat has still not been paid for.) At the suggestion of Matthew Mugg, the Doctor joins Blossom's circus, together with his animal family, Matthew, and Matthew's wife, Theodosia.

Almost immediately, the Doctor runs afoul of the circus people. He wants to put an end to the false advertising ("The Greatest Show on Earth"). He protests the Princess Fatima's treatment of her snakes. He complains to Blossom about the treatment of the animals, but Blossom's response is set in purely economic terms: "'Why, Doc,' said he, 'if I was to do all the things you want me to I might as well leave the business! I'd be ruined'" (41–42). Dolittle decides not to leave the circus, only because he is convinced by the animals that his presence will be some kind of corrective.

The animals are soon proved right. Dolittle meets Sophie, who tells him a lamentable tale about her abduction from Alaskan waters and the subsequent pining away of her husband, who had been the leader of the seal colony. Dolittle resolves to help her escape, and with the help of Matthew's nimble fingers and the animals' distraction, Sophie escapes from the circus, meets Dolittle at the appointed spot, and begins her journey home. On the way, Dolittle puts off a pack of chasing hounds, disguises Sophie as an ill woman during a coach ride, helps her past mills and dams along the Kippet River, and finally gathers her up in his arms and throws her over a cliff into the sea.

But he is seen, and the presumption is that he has just murdered a woman and tried to hide her body. Thrown in jail, he is released when the judge, Sir William Peabody, recognizes him and believes his story. On the way home, Dolittle saves a vixen's family from Peabody's foxhounds and invents the "Dolittle Safety Pack," designed to help foxes escape from hounds.

On his return to the circus, he is more convinced than ever that he must effect reforms. At once he exposes a patent medicine scheme, leading to riots and the expulsion of the circus from Stowbury. He buys Fatima's snakes and threatens to leave the circus if she remains; she does not. And "he began to feel that his presence here was doing good" (247). The Doctor gains increased respect when he saves the circus by admitting to Blossom that he can talk to animals; the Doctor uses his linguistic skills to save the Talking Horse act, but he demands a price: Blossom must pension off Beppo, the old cart horse. Together, Beppo and the bespectacled horse first seen in *The Story of Doctor Dolittle* become the founding members of "The Retired Cab and Wagon Horses' Association."

Mr. Bellamy of Manchester sees Dolittle's skill with animals and invites the Blossom circus to appear with his own in Manchester. On the way to Manchester, Dolittle writes a play for his animal family, which they perform with great success. For the first time in his life, Dolittle becomes wealthy, but all is lost when the circus leaves Manchester, for Blossom absconds with the money, leaving the circus deeply in debt. The performers prevail upon Dolittle to become the manager, which he does; the circus is renamed, simply, the Dolittle Circus. Unlike any other circus, it makes no extravagant claims, has the various shows presided over by the animals themselves, takes excellent care of the animals' needs, and serves high tea in the afternoon. The Dolittle Circus is, the narrator notes, "more like a sort of family gathering than a strictly business matter" (379):

> There were no rules, or hardly any. And if little boys wanted to see "behind the scenes," or to go into the elephant's stall and pet him, they were personally conducted wherever they wished to go. This alone gave the circus a quality quite individual. And whenever the

wagon-train moved on its way, the children would follow
it for miles along the road and for weeks after would talk
of nothing but when it would come back again to visit
their town. For children everywhere were beginning to
regard the Dolittle Circus as something peculiarly their
own. (379)

The emphasis here on the children's reaction and their appropri-
ation of the circus to their own world establishes an enormous
distinction between the circus of Blossom and that of Dolittle.

And here the story ends. It is a curious ending, for there is no
real conclusion to the events. It is especially odd given that the
next novel in the sequence, *Doctor Dolittle's Zoo,* does not take up
where *Doctor Dolittle's Circus* leaves off. It seems that Lofting has
here written himself into something of a corner. Throughout the
novel the narrator has noted how in time the Dolittle Circus became well known, its various acts well recognized. But at the conclusion of the novel the circus has only just been established. By
leaving the conclusion open-ended—by assigning no terminus to
the travels of the Dolittle Circus—Lofting allows for the time it
would take to establish the reputation that the narrator has been
hinting at all along.

As the title suggests, the locus of this novel's action is a circus.
In the same way that Lofting used the post office houseboat to
center his plot situations in *Doctor Dolittle's Post Office,* he uses
the circus wagon to center the situations of *Doctor Dolittle's Circus.* The wagon is movable like the houseboat, and it too establishes a home for Dolittle and his animal family. It also connotes
adventure and travel at the same time that it suggests the cozy
warmth of a home. It is the perfect setting for Gub-Gub.

Gub-Gub used to boast that . . . he was a born traveler,
that he loved change, like the Doctor. As a matter of fact,
he was really by nature much more like Dab-Dab; for no
one loved regular habits, especially regular meals, more
than he. It was just that the gipsy life provided a continuous and safe sort of adventure for him. He liked excite-

ment, but comfortable excitement, without hardship or danger. (309)

Here the circus wagon becomes a physical extension of Dolittle himself, who is ever ready to welcome change, ever eager to begin the next journey, to peer intently and hardily through the arch of experience. But unlike Tennyson's Ulysses, he is not one to welcome hardship as if it were itself a virtue. He will face it nonplussed, with a razor and a top hat, waistcoat buttoned securely. In this context it is notable that the circus wagon, like the houseboat before, becomes known as a place where one might come to make tea (338).

The circus wagon, though it moves about in the physical world much more than the anchored houseboat, establishes a greater unity in the novel than the houseboat achieved in *Doctor Dolittle's Post Office*. Perhaps because it is intrinsically connected to animals, the circus wagon is a better locus for the plot situations. The result is that the disparate, episodic quality of *Doctor Dolittle's Post Office* is missing here; the events are knit—though not tightly—by their uniform connection to the world of the circus. The only departure from this unity is the story of Sophie's escape, though here too the story begins and ends in the circus wagon.

This clear locus helps to establish the major theme of the novel: the disturbing distinction between how animals are treated and how they should be treated. This had been a minor melody in the first three Dolittle novels, sometimes emerging as a primary melody. But in *Doctor Dolittle's Circus* it swells to a full crescendo, almost obliterating any other concern. From this novel to the end of the series, this will be one of the foremost themes. And yet the seriousness of the theme will be consistently subdued by the gentle fantasy of the Dolittle adventures. The Dolittle books may have begun with atrocities against horses, and Lofting may have turned to Dolittle as a kind of therapeutic mode, but the therapy Dolittle offers is not anger, not a dramatic call. It is instead a charming yet insistent suggestion that one should look at animals from their own perspective, and look with humane eyes.

This concern is consistently worked out in the plot situations
of the novel. Where the situations of the first three novels had
been episodic, often inspired by chance and circumstance, the situations of *Doctor Dolittle's Circus* all deal with intended improve-
ments in the conditions of the animals. This is what leads Dolittle
to stay in the circus, though he is disgusted by its deceits. This is
what drives the action of the novel: how will Dolittle succeed in
bettering the menagerie conditions? This is what leads to the logical conclusion of the novel, where Lofting pushes past even the
benevolent management of Dolittle to the point where the animals themselves run their individual acts.

The theme is announced early on, as Dolittle returns from his
African voyage: "[A]lthough the people in Puddleby had not yet
learned of the Doctor's arrival, news of this coming had already
spread among the animals, and the birds. And all that afternoon
he was kept busy bandaging, advising, and physicking, while a
huge motley crowd of creatures waited patiently outside the surgery door" (4). Dab-Dab remarks that it is "just like old times" (4),
but she is not quite right—the absolute absorption of the Doctor's
time goes beyond anything in the earlier novels. What is remarkable is Dolittle's acceptance of the demands. There is nothing here
of what will come in later novels, when Dolittle yearns to escape
the same demands he cheerfully accepts here.

As with later novels, particularly *Doctor Dolittle's Zoo* and *Doctor Dolittle and the Green Canary,* Lofting will place the Doctor
in situations where he challenges a kind of institutional neglect
and abuse of animals. When he first arrives at Blossom's circus,
he goes to see the menagerie: "It was a dingy third-rate sort of
collection. Most of the animals seemed dirty and unhappy. The
Doctor was so saddened he was all for having a row with Blossom
over it" (30). He resists, on the advice of Matthew Mugg, but because Lofting wishes to establish the concern that will structure
the entire novel, Dolittle is not allowed to resist for long. At the
end of the first day he goes back to the menagerie and listens to
the animals' complaints: "[T]heir cages were not kept properly
clean; they did not get exercise or room enough; with some the
food served was not the kind they liked" (41). Though the Doctor

is indignant, he can do nothing for them at this point. By the end of the novel, all of these complaints will have been remedied and the basic assumptions of the institution—that circus animals exist only to perform for the delight of human spectators—will have been overturned.

The other challenge comes during the account of the fox hunt. Dolittle has just been released from prison and the threat of a murder trial when he comes upon a vixen and her cubs. The narrator emphasizes the vixen's motherliness: she is proud of her cubs but concerned with one's speed. The illustration depicting the moment when Dolittle diagnoses the cub's flat feet suggests the vixen's concern, as she looks on anxiously during the examination. The rounded tree, the overhead branch, the bent back of the Doctor, the Doctor's benign smile and handling of the exposed cub—all establish a secure moment.

But that is destroyed—actually in midsentence—by the sound of the horn. The vixen's distress is pictured in animal terms, yet it also echoes a human parent's concern.

> "Oh, what shall I do?" she moaned. "The children! If it wasn't for them I could perhaps give the dogs the slip. Oh, why did I bring them out in daylight to see you? I suppose I was afraid you might be gone if I waited till after dark. Now I've left our scent behind us, all the way from Broad Meadows, as plain as the nose on your face. And I've come right into the wind. What a fool I was! What shall I do? What shall I do?" (198)

The despair is evident in the shortened, disconnected sentences, the panic not allowing for any responses. Even if she were alone she would not necessarily escape; with her children, one of whom is quite slow, she is certainly trapped.

The hunters are pictured in a darkly comic tone. Their excitement, their concern over a single fox, the ludicrous scene of horses and hounds thundering upon a single fox—all are the stuff of comic opera: "'My goodness!' murmured the Doctor. 'Was there ever anything so childish? All this fuss for a poor little fox!'" (202).

But there is a darkness here as well; the hounds leap in together for a kill. From their point of view they are justified: "[T]hey eat rabbits and chickens, you know" (204). But for the human beings, the rending of the vixen would be nothing but sport. Dolittle himself never articulates anger at this; nor does the narrator. But Dolittle's repetition of his evaluation of the sport—"perfectly childish" (205)—carries more than a bemused dismissal. It is a condemnation of a practice emblematic of how human beings treat animals—and how such treatment shrivels the humanity of those who practice it.

One is always clearly on the side of the animals in a Dolittle book, particularly given the narrator's emphasis on Dolittle's perspective. But at the same time, the character of Dolittle is constantly encouraging another kind of reading: one from the animals' perspective. This is not a perspective that the narrator will take up, but the reader is certainly led to it by Dolittle. (One is tempted to say that this is also Lofting's perspective, but to do so is to run the danger of reducing the Dolittle novels to mere moral tales.)

This perspective emerges in a chapter entitled "The Perfect Pasture"; its perfection lies in the perspective of Beppo and the old plow horse:

> "The place I've always dreamed of," said Beppo, gazing across the landscape with a wistful look in his old eyes, "is like this—part of it is sloping and part of it is flat. Slopes are such a nice change: the grass is nearer to your nose, and the flats are restful to get back to after the slopes. Then it has trees, big spreading trees with fat trunks—the kind horses love to stand under and think— after a hearty meal. It has a copse where herbs and wild roots grow, the sorts we love to nibble for a change—especially wild mint, which is soothing to the stomach when you've eaten too much. It has good water—not a muddy, little pond, but a decent brook where the water is always sparkling and clear. In a hollow it has a nice

old shelter with a dry floor and a mossy, tiled roof that doesn't let the rain in. The pasture varies: some places are firm, croppy turf; others are deep, luscious, long hay-grass with buttercups and fragrant wild flowers mixed in it. At the top of the hilly part you can get a view of the sunsets to the westward and the south. And on the summit there is a good firm post to scratch your neck on. I love to watch the sun go down as I scratch my neck of an evening. The whole place is protected with good fences from snappy dogs and worrisome people. It is quiet. It is peaceful." (287–288)

This is Beppo's description of the place where he would like to spend his retirement. Everything in it is from the eye of an old horse, interpreted according to the horse's needs. When it turns out that such a place exists, the reader looks at it from Beppo's perspective: "Here, facing the sunny southward, they looked over a farm-gate into the loveliest meadow you ever saw" (288). It is lovely, however, because it exactly matches the description Beppo has just given, including a post for Beppo to scratch his neck on. The reader's affirmation of the spot—and the Doctor's—comes about because of the extent to which it has matched Beppo's vision. The reader too sees the meadow through the animal's perspective. It is perhaps Lofting's moment of greatest narrative skill, where the structure of the text becomes its theme.

Still, the question of the narrator is still not completely resolved in this novel. Lofting has not yet returned to Stubbins, and so the source of the narrative voice is unclear. "This is the story of that part of Doctor Dolittle's adventures which came about through his joining and traveling with a circus," the opening announces (1). And the stance of the narrator here is similar to the stance Dolittle himself assumes as he tells stories to the animals grouped around the fireside: "Well, the point from which we are beginning, then, is where the Dolittle party . . . had returned at last to the little house in Puddleby-on-the-Marsh after their long journey from Africa" (2). The stance is informal, an attempt to simulate an oral setting. The difficulty comes with the anonymity of the informal narrator—unless one assumes that the narrator is meant to be Lofting himself.

Despite the anonymity, the narrator is a strong presence in the novel. Some of this strength comes from a continuity of presence that is missing in the other Dolittle novels; this narrator rarely yields to another voice. There are no extended framed tales here, stories of Columbus's rescue or Noah's flood. The only tale the narrator does not recount is the story of Sophie's abduction from Alaska; this story is put into the seal's mouth. But her narrative is short, and it is constantly being interrupted by Dolittle's own questions. There are none of the protracted tales in which Dolittle plays no part; this is one of the few novels in which this will be true.

The narrator also asserts a strong presence through the frequent asides, the brief interludes where the action is commented on. In the middle of Sophie's escape, the narrator interrupts the flow of the action to look ahead.

> "The second half of his adventures with Sophie, in which none of his own animals took part, came, indeed, to be a favorite tale with the Dolittle fireside circle for many, many years—particularly one chapter. And whenever the animals were feeling in need of a cheerful yarn they always pestered the Doctor to re-tell them that part of his elopement with the seal which Gub-Gub called "the Grantchester Coach." But we are going ahead of our story. (120–22)

Here the narrator has intruded very obviously by breaking into the plot situation. The passage forms a transition between the two halves of the escape attempt, but it also subverts any suspense: we know from this that the escape will end happily and even, perhaps, comically. The plural pronouns in the final sentence suggest a switch of narrator and reader, again stressing the narrator's presence and again simulating an oral retelling: the reader too comes out of the immediacy of the story to view it for a moment as what it is—a story.

At other times the narrator will break in for other reasons. Later, during Sophie's escape, the narrator hints at a coming event: "It was not until some time afterward, when the Doctor revisited his old friend—in a way you will hear of later on—that he learned the story of that return journey which the plow horse made alone" (165). During the animal plays the narrator will break in to remind the reader of Dolittle's fictional accomplishments, establishing a context of reality to the fantasy: "Doctor Dolittle had, as you know, written plays before for animals—dozens of them. . . . But all these had been intended for audiences of animals and were written in animal languages" (311). Here again the narrator reaches for the complicity of the reader: "as you know." And at times the narrator will enter to establish his own rather intimate knowledge of the Dolittle household: "In the course of their eventful lives the animals of Doctor Dolittle's household had had many exciting times. But I doubt if anything ever happened to them which they remembered longer or spoke of afterward more often than their first appearance before the public in the famous Puddleby Pantomime" (330). The kind of intimacy reflected here suggests the presence of a narrator like Stubbins, a suggestion to be fulfilled in subsequent novels.

One implication of this intimate narrator and of the revelation of who that narrator is in *Doctor Dolittle's Zoo* is that the Dolittle novels do not stand as 12 individual volumes. While in some series this may be a structural flaw, in the Dolittle series it is a strength. Lofting creates here not so much a set of independent adventures—in fact, they are not independent—as a world, a gentle world where the impossible has happened: animals and human beings can speak. The reader is not dropped into 12 isolated moments in the history of that world, as a reader is in L. Frank Baum's *Oz* books. The reader instead begins with Dolittle's entrance into a new vision of the animal world in *The Story of Doctor Dolittle* and continues to follow the unfolding of the implications and complexities of that vision.

The result is that each of the volumes contains frequent references to past volumes, a technique that connects the volumes strongly together. *Doctor Dolittle's Circus* refers to the voyage from Africa with the Pushmi-Pullyu from *The Story of Doctor Dolittle* (2), as well as the bespectacled horse from the same novel, who here plays a much more prominent role and is even named for the first time. The novel also refers to the gull who warned Dolittle about the Cape Stephen Light in *Doctor Dolittle's Post Office*. Too-Too remarks, "I hadn't seen him since the good old houseboat days" (60). In these cases the references are evocative, recalling old plot situations and suggesting a motive for the animals' willingness to help Dolittle: they owe him for past favors. At times the references are too incidental to work well, however. Twice in the novel Dolittle meets his sister, Sarah, last seen in *The Story of Doctor Dolittle*. She rebukes him for his working at a circus and surprises him during Sophie's escape. At neither time does her presence contribute to the plot situation; nor does the reference to her serve to evoke useful connotations or images. This reference, at least, is merely gratuitous.

In a series, such references might be expected. But what is particularly strong in the Dolittle series is the evocation of elements that become very familiar as the reader moves from text to text, the standard elements of the novels that reappear with comfortable consistency. In *Doctor Dolittle's Circus* Dolittle is, as ever, the selfless fellow who will not seek wealth: "Money! Bah! It's a curse," he exclaims (275). And when he takes over the management of the circus, he establishes a kind of benevolent socialism, where any profits are shared equally, according to the contribution of the worker.

As always, the Dolittle garden is in the background. Although Lofting will eventually devote an entire novel to this setting, here it stands as a kind of paradise where there are no watchful dragons but the ones set up by one's own busyness. It is one of Dolittle's most natural settings. Even while escaping with Sophie, he takes the time to prune a garden: "'Dear me!' he said, tiptoeing back to the shed for a hoe and a basket. 'What a shame to neglect a fine place like this!'" (100). And soon he is weeding and pruning, "just as though the garden were his own and no danger threatened him within a thousand miles" (100).

The tending of the garden, so important in Victorian and Edwardian children's novels, becomes an emblem of Dolittle's self-assurance, peacefulness, and placidity. Its nature is an extension of his own nurturing character. And the garden itself becomes an emblem of England, still seen in Lofting's expatriate vision as one large garden: "It is certainly most delightful country, this," murmurs the Doctor (194). And it is, filled with brooks and meadows, sloping fields, and small villages named Appledyke. Lofting, writing soon after the Great War, pictures a world untouched by anything mean. It is a world that Dolittle could attend at any turn, and indeed this drive will become stronger and stronger as the series progresses.

Doctor Dolittle's Zoo

Doctor Dolittle's Zoo was published in 1928, the fifth in a series that had begun only five years previously. Any series, particularly one dependent on its previous volumes, as is the Dolittle series, will have volumes that seem pedestrian, carried along by the sheer momentum of the series as well as the strong central characters. And so it is with *Doctor Dolittle's Zoo*. This novel creaks and groans mightily as it is pushed into line. Perhaps the least unified of all the novels, it is carried principally by the strength of Stubbins the narrator and the presence of the Doctor, though in the end Dolittle plays rather a small role in the actual plot situations of the novel.

Any series runs the risks of overdoing an idea, particularly one that is so dependent on the strength of the actual character. Some series, like Eleanor Estes's Moffat series, Louise Fitzhugh's Harriet series, or Susan Cooper's *The Dark Is Rising* series, work against this potential weakening by varying the prominence of individual characters from novel to novel. But for Lofting, Dolittle was the series. Though Stubbins would become increasingly important and though Lofting could include more and more framed

tales, eventually allowing such tales to dominate, he always kept
Dolittle in view—sometimes distanced, but clearly in view. For an
author writing so quickly, this is not hard to understand.

The reviewer for the *New York Times Book Review* hinted at
Lofting's prodigious production of Dolittle books. "[W]ith each one
of the successive volumes," the reviewer claimed, "the wonder has
grown that he could keep up the pace he had set in the first and
that invention, fancy, whimsical humor, incidents, evolving story,
should continue to bubble forth from his pen with as much grace
and charm and freshness as in the beginning."[10] This would be a
wonder, but the reviewer was too enthusiastic. (This review begins with the astonishing claim that "[n]ever, since man began to
make books, have there been so many and such beautiful books
for young readers.") Much of the material of this novel, particularly the framed tales, are whimsical and perhaps even inventive,
but Lofting's literary powers are not high here in terms of his
placement of these tales in the context of an entire novel. A successful novel does not come from a series of tales that have bub-
bled from a pen and then been juxtaposed. The wonder here is not
that Lofting has continued to produce tales but that *Doctor Dolittle's Zoo* does not fail as a novel. Whimsy is not enough, and
Lofting, if not the reviewer, understood that.

Doctor Dolittle's Zoo begins—in terms of its plot—directly following *The Voyages of Doctor Dolittle*; in fact, the Doctor returns
to the shore to bid farewell to the Sea Snail. As the party watches
the Great Sea Snail move slowly out to sea, they sense that they
are truly back in England, home from the exotic settings of the
preceding three years. (And indeed there will be nothing close to
an exotic setting anywhere in this novel.) They are greeted by two
ducks who have seen them land and who bring a message from
Dab-Dab: they are to carry home some groceries, evidence that,
for Dab-Dab, domesticity is to be prized above all else.

While Dolittle returns home, Stubbins, the narrator of this
novel, heads into town to gather the supplies. He is pleased and
surprised to find that few people recognize him; three years is a
long time for a young boy. He envisions himself as the great adventurer returning home, the fulfillment of those dreams he had

dreamed at the opening of *The Voyages of Doctor Dolittle,* when he had sat on the bridge and imagined traveling to foreign lands. And so he has, and now he has returned as more than a mere apprentice. In this novel he will begin to grow into a true assistant to the Doctor.

When Stubbins returns, he finds that he has not missed the household's welcome: they have donned their costumes from *Doctor Dolittle's Circus* and throw a grand welcoming party. At its conclusion the Doctor sits by the fireside and recounts the adventures of the voyages, setting the pattern for the rest of this novel, in which many characters tell stories. The next day, Dolittle settles into his practice and inspects the garden. Resolving to establish a zoo to be designed and run by animals, he places Stubbins in charge and turns to the accumulated notebooks of the voyages.

Soon the zoo is established. Designed to accommodate several "neighborhoods," it includes homes for mice and rats, mixed-breed dogs, badgers, foxes, and squirrels—all animals native to England, for, Dolittle reasons, the climate is not healthy for animals not born to it. The animals all agree to abandon their predatory habits while inside the zoo: "And it was surprising how, when the danger of pursuit by their natural enemies was removed, all the different sorts of animals took up a new, freer and more open kind of life."[11] Of course, the expense is enormous and the household is saved only by a chance finding of some abandoned gold nuggets.

When Dolittle invents a written alphabet for the mouse language, he and Stubbins begin to record tales from mice and to bind these into books for a mouse and rat library. These tales of hardship overcome by resourceful mice take up much of the remainder of the book. It will also be a mouse that propels Dolittle into the search for a lost will at Moorsden Manor. In conducting that search, Dolittle is forced into dealing with his neighbors— something exceedingly distasteful for him—in order to save a mouse family from a fire. In so doing, he uncovers a will that an heir had wished to suppress, for most of the estate's money had been left to a society for the prevention of cruelty to animals. The novel concludes with a great festival held in celebration of the fortune that will benefit the animal world.

The kinds of stories included in *Doctor Dolittle's Zoo* are familiar to a reader who has already worked through other books in the series. But there is a significant difference between this novel and *Doctor Dolittle's Post Office* and *Doctor Dolittle's Circus*: the narrative stance. Here, as in *The Voyages of Doctor Dolittle*, Stubbins is the narrator, though his perspective is different from that of the earlier novel. At the beginning of *Doctor Dolittle's Zoo*, Stubbins is no longer a nine-year-old-boy; nor is he even the 12-year-old boy who participates in the plot situations of the novel. "Already I see gray hairs showing at your temples, Tommy. If you try to write down everything the Doctor did, you'll be nearly my age before you've finished," Polynesia gently chides him (2). And so this novel is, ostensibly, written by an older narrator looking back on his past, though the perspective he assumes in the actual plot is that of someone living in the present, watching events unfold even as the reader watches.

When Stubbins announces to the parrot that he is going to begin another book of Dolittle's memoirs, Polynesia is astonished: "'Another!' she exclaimed. 'Is there going to be another Dolittle book?'" (1). She then wonders who will decide how many Dolittle books will come out, and Stubbins replies that "in the end—the public does" (1). Here Lofting the author is a bit too intrusive and actually makes Stubbins speak erroneously. In the world of the novels—in which Stubbins and Polynesia exist—the parrot is the one to make the decisions on how many books there shall be. She promises to be his critic and editor. She is the one who poses the problem that besets all biographers: "There is so much of interest in the life of John Dolittle that the problem is what to leave out, rather than what to put in" (1–2).

The reference to memoirs is significant, in that it suggests Stubbins's attitude toward his task. That he is writing "another book of Doctor Dolittle's memoirs" (1) establishes him as the apparent author of the earlier novels, in three of which he played no part. He sees his task as one of biography, but his choice of the word *memoir* complicates the task. Memoirs are recorded memories, generally recorded by the person whose memories they are. In a sense Stubbins is writing memoirs, but they are his own, in which the Doctor figures prominently. Almost unconsciously Stubbins is actually writing about his own life, making the reader see Dolittle through Stubbins's own eyes.

Any book in a series faces the obstacle of overcoming the break between it and the previous novel. *Doctor Dolittle's Zoo* overcomes this break by using a fictive metafiction. When Stubbins announces the title, Polynesia gives advice on the novel's structure: "Then I suppose you ought to get on to the zoo part as soon as possible. But first I think you had better put in a little about your own homecoming and your parents and all that. You *had* been away nearly three years, you know. Of course it's sort of sentimental. But some people like a little sentiment in their books" (3). Stubbins follows this advice to a point; he eliminates the sentiment by eliminating any reference to his own first visit to his parents. But he does begin by recalling the conclusion of *The Voyages of Doctor Dolittle,* thereby orienting the reader in terms of the novels' sequence.

The result of Stubbins's narrative presence is a very different stance toward the action. Tommy is the first-person narrator, but he is also a participant in the novel's action. The reader experiences that action from the consciousness of the narrator, making the experience of the plot situations immediate and vivid: "If it had not been for Jip's good guidance we would have had a hard job to make our way to the town across the marshes. The light of the late afternoon was failing. And every once in a while the fog would come billowing in from the sea and blot out everything around us, so that you could see no further than a foot before your nose. The chimes of the quarter-hours from Puddleby church tower were the only sounds or signs of civilization to reach us" (8–9). The ability to organize such images into a full setting, together with the ability to use a list of descriptive details to establish a tone, is a narrative stance uniquely Tommy's; there is nothing quite like it in any of the other Dolittle books that do not use Stubbins as a narrator. Lofting has here found his proper, most effective form. And though this form will set up a mediating presence between the reader and the character of Dolittle, Lofting will craft Stubbins in such a way that he is both intrinsically interesting himself (he is not merely a flat recorder of events, not Dolittle's Boswell) and a vantage point from which we get the perspective of a child on someone whom the child sees as a great man. The success of Stubbins as a narrator comes through Lofting's ability to use Stubbins's perspective to simultaneously distance the Doctor (he is a great man who is not always to be disturbed) and to bring the reader closer to the action of the novel by using a child's point of view.

The central image of the prologue—Stubbins bent over his notebooks, writing as Polynesia watches—matches the image of the prologue to *The Voyages of Doctor Dolittle*. Polynesia's presence next to the narrator links Dolittle and Stubbins together and brings the past into the present and the present back into the past. Polynesia perched next to Stubbins the naturalist (which he soon will become) is only the expected succession from Polynesia perched next to Dolittle the naturalist. The prologues of both books suggest that Stubbins will eventually take over for Dolittle, though that change will never actually be seen in the plot situations of the novels—nor is it to be expected, given that the novels, from Lofting's perspective but also from Stubbins's, are about the Doctor.

Still, the novels do chronicle Stubbins's growth. And he is the character in the series who changes the most. Doctor Dolittle himself seems permanent and unchanging; his stolid good humor and habitual tranquillity are as fixed as the primum mobile. But Stubbins is quite different. Through the course of the novels he becomes not only the apprentice but the successor of the Doctor. And it is this change that gives reality to his character. In this fantasy world where men can talk to both animals and plants, Lofting inserts a character who grows up in a realistic sense. In this growth Stubbins finds the true fulfillment of his dreams, a fulfillment even more marvelous than trips to unimagined places: he finds a vocation.

In *Doctor Dolittle's Zoo* Stubbins is still clearly the young apprentice. Sent into town to buy sausages, he finds that he can only pay with a Spanish silver piece. When the butcher refuses to accept it, Stubbins eyes him with sore disdain and announces

that he is shopping for Doctor Dolittle: "I said this with the su-
perior air of an experienced traveler, raising my eyebrows a little
disdainfully at the obstinate butcher, whose stay-at-home mind
couldn't be expected to appreciate a real adventurer's difficulties"
(14). The butcher smiles at his "airs" (14), an appropriate response of the adult world looking with some humor at the pretensions of the child world. Stubbins here is one whose authority
comes through association; he has not yet begun to establish himself as a naturalist—or as an adult—in his own right. Consequently, the focus of this novel is still fixed principally on Dolittle,
though later novels will begin to examine Stubbins's own skills as
a naturalist and veterinarian.

Still, *Doctor Dolittle's Zoo* does show at least the beginnings of
Stubbins's growing responsibilities and skills, as Dolittle asks
him, with the help of Polynesia, to "plan out the new zoo for me"
(36). It falls to Stubbins to lay out the structure of the zoo that
will be the setting for the novel. His response shows his own jus-
tifiable pride—"I felt very proud that the Doctor had intrusted
such a large measure of the responsibility to me" (36)—but it is
tempered by the recognition that the entire conception of the zoo
was Dolittle's.

The zoo is set on several acres in the back part of the garden, a
setting to which Dolittle has gladly returned. Earlier novels
touched on Dolittle's love of his garden, his joy in its cultivation,
his pleasure in its bound privacy. It is one of the first places he
examines on his return. He is overwhelmed by its three-year neglect: "He almost wept as he stepped out of the kitchen door and
saw the desolation of it fully revealed in the bright morning sun-
light" (29). Seeing him, the birds who have waited all night
swarm around him, reminding Stubbins of pictures of St.
Frances—an apt image for one so close to the animal world; it is
almost surprising that Lofting waited until the fifth novel to use
it, though it comes, appropriately, from a narrator who would be
likely to make such connections.

The endpapers of the novel—unhappily lost in later editions—
picture Dolittle serenely seated in his garden. He poses in a scene
that Tommy might be observing, surrounded by his animal fam-

ily, secure in the walled garden, still—for the moment—and at
peace. Such stillness is a rarity in a Dolittle novel, and it matches
the restricted, bound setting of the novel's action. No other novel
will be as unified in terms of its setting. No other novel will focus
so exclusively on life in such a bound setting. In this sense the
garden is the literary descendant of the houseboat of *Doctor Dolittle's Post Office* and the carnival wagon of *Doctor Dolittle's
Circus.*

A theme that had been implicit in these two earlier novels
grows much more explicit in *Doctor Dolittle's Zoo*: how should humanity live, both with itself and in accord with the animal world?
The Dolittle series began with an emphasis principally on the latter, but as the series developed its focus shifted so that, covered
with the humorous whimsy of the plots, Lofting included his vision of what humanity ought to be. This vision will become more
and more explicit until *Doctor Dolittle in the Moon,* still three
years away. Here, though, Lofting establishes a world that becomes an emblem of how humanity might live, a world free from
predation, where animals consciously hold back their oppressive
natures (the existence of which is never denied) to live together
for the general betterment of the whole. In the end, they rejoice
that a benefactor has been found for the entire animal world, not
just a single element in it. By implication, Lofting critiques humanity's inability to live in accord with itself.

When the Prison Rat comes to tell his story, it has implications
for this theme. Caught in an empty pail, the rat is about to be
destroyed by the artist inhabiting the studio that is the story's
setting. But the artist does not kill the rat, muttering, "Oh
well . . . I suppose your life means something to you" (183). And
indeed it does. The two become fast friends; when the artist is
arrested, the rat searches until he finds him in prison—caught as
he had once been caught—and shows him how to escape. But the
other rats cannot understand this relationship: "They didn't trust
Humans, they said, considering them a low-down, cruel and
deceitful race, not in any way to be compared with rats for frank-
ness and honesty" (186). Now these are not the Houyhnhnms of

Gulliver's Travels; however, had the tone been just a bit harsher these rats would not be far from that race.

But the artist and the Prison Rat have overcome mutual distrust by recognizing that each has a life that is meaningful; in this mutual recognition, peace is established. This is the prime element of Doctor Dolittle's zoo: "For instance, it was no unusual thing in Animal Town to see a mother squirrel lolling on her veranda, surrounded by her children, while a couple of terriers walked down the street within a yard of them" (45). It is a world of astonishing peace, though outside of its walled boundaries predators still roam.

Yet this too is a part of Dolittle's plan: to see if the harmony established between creatures in the zoo could be generalized beyond the garden: "Obviously, Stubbins, . . . we can't expect foxes to give up their taste for spring chickens, or dogs their love of ratting, all in a moment. My hope is that by getting them to agree to live peaceably together while within my zoo, we will tend toward a better understanding among them permanently" (48). Now this is all part of the delicate fantasy, and Lofting, gentle idealist that he was, is not calling for the impossible: to change en masse the very nature of the animal kingdom. But behind the fantasy is the hope—later to become more explicit—that humanity could do what is being done in the zoo.

When the first "mooniversary" dinner is held at the Rat and Mouse Club, the white mouse addresses the audience; the Doctor and Stubbins are in attendance. The mouse rejoices in the advances the mice have been able to effect given the existence of the zoo. "What has our life always been heretofore?" he asks. "Why, getting chased, being hunted—flight, concealment, that was our daily lot" (104)—a description not particularly inappropriate for a writer who spent a war huddled in trenches behind fields of barbed wire. The mice now enjoy a "comfortable peace and honest freedom" (105), the result of Dolittle's work. This passage is not overtly didactic—those passages will come in later novels—but it does emphasize the major recurring theme of *Doctor Dolittle's Zoo.*

This novel is especially important in the Dolittle series for its more explicit introduction of the theme of how humanity should live. It also continues some familiar patterns. As with other books, this one contains references to earlier novels, particularly *The Voyages of Doctor Dolittle* and *Doctor Dolittle's Circus,* the two novels that directly precede *Doctor Dolittle's Zoo* in terms of the chronological time of the characters. This novel continues to use episodic adventures and framed tales, some of which, like those of previous novels, are not particularly anchored in the plot situations of the novel. The Doctor and his animal household maintain their long-established characters. And events consistently reach toward the implausible; they always seem about to escape the controls of the gentle and reasonable Doctor, and yet always work out for the good. (One episode is startlingly weak, however: when the household needs money, Stubbins and Polynesia dig up several gold nuggets on Puddleby Common that had apparently been accidentally dropped there long ago. This calls for too great a suspension of disbelief).

And Stubbins has returned, though his prologue would suggest that he has never left. He would not be present in all of the remaining novels; he would be missing from the next and from one published after Lofting's death, a novel Lofting had not fully crafted and structured. But Stubbins's reappearance is important for this novel, as it would be for subsequent novels. His narrative voice, character growth, and position as a mediator between the reader and Doctor Dolittle all contribute to the strength of the novel.

Doctor Dolittle's Caravan

The year 1926 saw the release of yet another Dolittle book, *Doctor Dolittle's Caravan*; the things were coming as regularly as clockwork. But regularity is rarely to be prized in the writing of novels, and it is not to be prized in this one. Although *Doctor Dolittle's Caravan* would not prove to be the weakest of the Dolittle novels, it would certainly stake a claim for that unenviable spot. Almost alone of all the Dolittle books it shows a lack of consistent purpose and a want of invention that single it out as hackwork.

If those are harsh words for this novel, they would have seemed harsher still if said in the mid-1920s, when the Dolittle books created that kind of mythical world which, librarians and critics seemed to assume, children willingly participated in. It hardly seemed right to criticize such a gentle, wholesome world as that established by Lofting. All the more remarkable, then, are the words of Marcia Dalphin, reviewing *Doctor Dolittle's Caravan* for the *New Republic*. Much of her review explores the question of what specifically attracts children to these books. She concludes that it is Lofting's "vigorous imagination and inexhaustible invention," as well as "[t]he staunch little figure of Doctor Dolittle himself."[12]

But then she turns to the novel at hand, where, she concludes, "[t]he charm of the earlier volumes is lacking. The author is not as happy in his bird characters as in his animals. There are many dull pages. Nor are the faults so evident in the other books overcome." Those faults, she suggests, consist of "more commonplace and colloquial language than the characterizations call for" and "plays to the adult gallery." The latter a child reader will simply skip over, and they are so infrequent in the novel as to be hardly called a fault. (Lofting would see them as integral to the tone of the book.) The colloquial language is similarly not a special problem; here Dalphin is referring to Matthew Mugg and Cheapside, both exaggerated Cockney characters. Their humor comes from their exaggerated language, which matches their exaggerated characters.

The principal problem with the novel lies not in those two difficulties but in Dalphin's simple assertion: "There are many dull pages." There are indeed. Aside from a single prolonged incident in which Dolittle burglarizes a pet shop, the novel creeps, a pastiche of less-than-suspenseful incidents that, had they been fully developed, might have been comic. Dalphin concludes her review with a warning to Lofting: "If anyone has been able to make a dent in the theory of the critical high hats that books in series tend to become ever more and more attenuated in interest it is

Hugh Lofting. . . . He must have a care, however, for even the appealing little round medical gentleman from Puddleby-on-the-Marsh who gave up his practice to become an animal doctor cannot withstand the assaults of too long an exploitation." The irony in this warning is that it is sounded too late.

Doctor Dolittle's Caravan begins at the end of *Doctor Dolittle's Circus*; one almost has the feeling that this is material left over from that earlier novel. Passing a pet shop, Dolittle and Matthew Mugg hear a beautiful song from a female canary, the sex reputed not to sing. Entranced, they purchase her and listen that night to the story of her life, told in song and verse. Dolittle, looking for a new act for his circus, decides on a canary opera, which will use this canary (named Pippinella) as the diva; her life story will be the libretto.

As they travel to London, the Doctor rehearses Pippinella and recruits more birds for the chorus. They also prepare the Puddleby Pantomime, which had been so successful in Manchester in *Doctor Dolittle's Circus*. Searching for a leading male singer, Matthew Mugg and Pippinella visit London's pet shops; there they find Twink, Pippinella's lost mate, in a dreary, stuffy shop.

Aghast at the conditions in that shop (which sold wild birds that had been trapped), Dolittle disguises himself and, together with Matthew, breaks into the shop and frees all the wild birds, as well as two dogs that eventually come to the Dolittle circus. The Doctor is able to put off the proprietor's anger when one of the freed dogs reveals Mr. Harris's handling of stolen goods. This scene, right at the center of the novel, is the one moment of true invention and sparkling action.

The opera is performed in London, and though many critics do not know what to make of a bird opera, the interest of Paganini is enough to ensure that it will be discussed—and that crowds will come. The troupe is lionized in London, and the animals become much sought after as advertisements to better animal conditions—better bird cages, for example. Eventually the animals all become wealthy enough to open their own bank accounts; the circus performers have also become wealthy through Dolittle's cooperative system of sharing profits. As the performers retire,

Dolittle decides to close the circus, sending the menagerie animals back to Africa. The fact that he will no longer serve peppermints to children is Dolittle's only regret as he leaves the circus life behind him.

But Lofting too has left something behind: a true conclusion to this novel. Throughout the novel Pippinella has been searching for her beloved former master, the window cleaner. This kind of search is common in the Dolittle books; in *Doctor Dolittle's Zoo* it appears in the story of the Prison Rat. And usually in the Dolittle books that search is fulfilled in some way. Here the search is simply dropped, one more story that couldn't be squeezed in somehow. Nor does Dolittle ever return to his garden, though not infrequent references to the garden have led the reader to expect this. Though the narrator suggests that *Doctor Dolittle's Caravan* is part of Dolittle's memoirs, it reads more like a journal, for it is not given the form and structure that would provide the various episodes with a contextual meaning.

This difficulty stems in part from the lack of Stubbins. Having returned to Stubbins as a narrator in *Doctor Dolittle's Zoo,* Lofting now lapses again into the anonymous third-person narrator for *Doctor Dolittle's Caravan.* Though the book's opening claim that it is a continuation of Dolittle's memoirs mirrors Stubbins's claim at the opening of *Doctor Dolittle's Zoo,* Stubbins's formative presence is missing; no one—certainly not the narrator—establishes any overall meanings for the novel. And while it is the case that Stubbins could not act as a character here, since the action takes place before he meets the Doctor, his mediating presence could still have unified the material in the novel and placed it in the context of the other Dolittle novels. As the novel stands, it is difficult to get past the sense that *Doctor Dolittle's Caravan* is a collection of tales that did not make it into *Doctor Dolittle's Circus* and that were to be more fully developed in *Doctor Dolittle and the Green Canary,* a book not published until 1950, after Lofting's death and under the editorship of Josephine Lofting and Olga Fricker.

There is much in *Doctor Dolittle's Caravan* that is familiar to readers of the series. Doctor Dolittle is unchanged, a fierce advocate of justice for the animal world, though gentle and easily moved. When Pippinella criticizes cats, Dolittle wonders "if that's what makes them the way they are . . . the fact that no one ever trusts them. It's a terrible strain on anybody's character."[13] It is almost outside the realm of possibility that Dolittle could imagine an animal with a bad nature.

Lofting typically refers to past novels, and such references do occur in *Doctor Dolittle's Caravan*. Sarah and her husband, the Reverend Dingle, surprise Dolittle in a disguise as he prepares to enter the pet shop he will plunder. Mr. Brown, reformed and no longer a quack vet, returns from *Doctor Dolittle's Circus,* having developed some real horse medicine. Even Sophia, the seal Dolittle helps to escape from Blossom's circus, is invoked. And once again Lofting uses the technique of the framed tale, here to allow Pippinella to tell the story of her life.

And again Lofting sets out the garden in Puddleby-on-the-Marsh as the ultimate haven for the Dolittle household. "Puddleby and the dear old house and garden have grown to be just a dream—just a dream," laments Dab-Dab (103–4). "My, but it will be good to see the old garden again! And the marketplace, and the bridge, and the river!" (220), muses Jip. Neither, however, will see the garden in this novel, not even after Cheapside brings the distressing news that it is all overgrown—just as in the opening of *Doctor Dolittle's Zoo*. There is just the faintest criticism here, the slightest suggestion, that Dolittle's wandering is not completely without reproach.

A final familiar element is Dolittle's perorations on how animals should be treated. Whereas this was a major unifying theme in *Doctor Dolittle's Zoo,* here the calls seem repetitive, tired, and worn. No new impetus or angle or meaning is given to this theme. "After all, our lives are our own even if we are dogs," asserts Toby (283), but this comes off more as a whine than an assertion of true independence. The Doctor believes that the animals should advertise to improve the general conditions of the animal kingdom. The animals are given bank accounts so that they might have power and status in the human world. After she is purchased by the Doctor, Pippinella rejoices that she is "once more among people who treated me like a friend, instead of just as something to be sold" (79). Dolittle rages against the trapping of wild birds and their deaths as they dash themselves against the cages in an effort to be free. But all of these occurrences are driven by the plot situations; they are not part of an overall meaning that invigorates and adds depth to those situations, as in *Doctor Dolittle's Zoo*.

This is not to say that there are no strengths to the novel. In the opening of the novel, Pippinella is developed as a strong character, although this characterization fades through the latter stages of the book. In the opening she is a plucky, proud bird who dares to drink out of Gub-Gub's bowl, "which piece of cheek greatly astonished that member of the household" (19). She is a survivor, one who endures great hardships and forms deep and lasting attachments—though circumstances always seem to separate her from those she loves. She is reflective: "Every once in a while I'd see a finch fly by and I'd get a sort of vague hankering to be out in the open, living a life of freedom. But one day I saw a hawk swoop down on a poor lame sparrow and carry him off. With a shudder I nestled down among my brothers and sisters and thanked my stars that I lived indoors" (36–37). This unusual perspective and her acceptance of circumstances give Pippinella her ability to survive.

The burglary scene is also strong in the novel. As Dolittle and Matthew are befuddled by their disguises and an unexpected policeman, Lofting's material swells with its old power. The humor and pathos of the freeing of the birds; Dolittle's righteous indignation against the shop owner, despite the fact that he is the one who is trespassing; the surprising physical aggression of Dolittle as he smacks a policeman and dives into the river; the utter poise and serenity with which he faces the potential consequences of his plundering—all are the stuff of the earlier novels. This scene is told with wit, suspense, and humor—Dolittle is daring and heroic and comic and awkward all at the same time, an uncommon juxtaposition of attributes that typifies Dolittle.

But Dalphin's criticism haunts this novel: "There are many dull pages." The opera—and preparation for it—consumes long chapters that have no action, no comedy, no dramatic interest. The members of the animal household seem weighed by a heavy hand, as if the narrator is deliberately preventing them from upstaging the canary. A chapter in which Jip accompanies Pippinella across London in search of her window cleaner is so sketchily written that one wonders if Jip has lost not only his sense of smell but his entire character.

The account of Pippinella's life has even more serious flaws. Lofting had been writing and publishing Pippinella's story in 1924 and 1925 for the *New York Herald Tribune* syndicate. Though he had intended to publish it as a separate volume, he instead attached some of that material to *Doctor Dolittle's Caravan*. It was an unfortunate attachment; since Dolittle's presence adds nothing to the story, the tale of Pippinella would have worked better as a novel outside of the Dolittle series. As part of *Doctor Dolittle's Caravan,* it is unwieldy, not fully incorporated into the narrative, and disproportionately emphasized.

Even the narrative stance of this section of the novel is confusing. After four chapters in which Pippinella tells her own story, the narrator seems to decide that the canary has been given too much space: "As I have already said, Pippinella's life was quite a long story. And since this book is to be a history of the Doctor's adventures, I feel it would be wiser if I told the rest of the contralto canary's career in my own words, rather than in the longer form in which she narrated it herself to the Dolittle household in the caravan" (52). What follows from here is a kind of cryptic summary of the canary's life, with such a rapid movement from incident to incident and such an unaccountable lack of transition and development as to suggest that these are notes for the longer stories in the *New York Herald Tribune.* Even the tenses are oddly inconsistent.

Following these instructions she finally came to Ebony Island, a jungle-covered mountainous piece of land only a few miles square. After she had recovered from her fatigue she examined the island and found it a pleasant enough place. She was treated kindly by the native birds, many cock finches vieing for her affections. But she is still too broken-hearted over her lover's faithlessness and she encourages none of them. She does not even tell them where she came from and she remains a sort of woman of mystery among the bird society of the island. (62–63)

The motiveless movement from the past tense to the present tense suggests that the author is unsure of what he wants this passage to be doing.

One final difficulty is the lack of a strong setting for this novel. All of the other novels in the series had centered on a place—Africa, a floating island, a houseboat, a zoo, a caravan wagon. Here the events center on a plot situation—the canary opera. This fails to tie all of the episodes together as the central settings had in the other novels. Perhaps it fails most acutely because Lofting fails to invest the opera with the inventive wit he had used with other plot situations. If the music critics in the novel are not sure what to make of the opera, neither in general is the child reader.

Perhaps a literary critic of this novel who points out its deficiencies is only trying to keep the high hat undented, to show that series do run out of inventiveness. Perhaps Lofting looks to his child audience to react in the same way that the children who heard Pippinella's opera reacted:

They were not nearly so concerned about their dignity and the importance of their musical opinion as were their elders. They laughed when they felt like laughing and drew in their breath with honest wonder when they were most impressed. They were delighted with the nest and particularly with the naughty member of the brood who was supposed to be Pippinella as a baby. And whenever she poked her nose out from under her mother's wing and tried to imitate her father's singing, the children just gurgled with merriment. Their laughter was catching and soon it had spread through the whole audience. (202)

Perhaps. But even so, this is not the book to dent the high hat.

Doctor Dolittle's Garden

It was not Hugh Lofting's practice to craft his Dolittle series in chronological order. In the same way that *Doctor Dolittle's Post Office* and *Doctor Dolittle's Circus* come between *The Voyages of Doctor Dolittle* and *Doctor Dolittle's Zoo,* so *Doctor Dolittle's Caravan* comes between *Doctor Dolittle's Zoo* and *Doctor Dolittle's Garden.* Like *Doctor Dolittle's Zoo, Doctor Dolittle's Garden* begins directly after the action of its companion novel. Both use Stubbins as the narrator. Both use the enclosed garden as a boundary for many of the plot situations. Both use animals who make their home in Doctor Dolittle's garden as narrators for extended tales.

At least one reviewer saw these similarities and took the line that most previous reviewers of the Dolittle books had taken: "Hugh Lofting's accounts of Doctor Doolittle's [*sic*] wonderful adventures and achievements have already become classics in the world of juvenile reading and the fact that they are greatly enjoyed by older people also is proof of their quality. Although this is the sixth [*sic*] of the series it shows no lessening in the power and fertility of his invention and his ability to make the most outlandish and amazing incidents and adventures seem realistic."[14] Most of this fortunately anonymous *New York Times* review is simple party line, spouted with little thought. What evidence suggests that the novels were popular with an adult audience? Is it possible for a series of books to become classic in any sense within seven years? Most definitions would suggest that a classic has stood at least the test of time. Do the incidents of this novel seem in any way realistic? Certainly this was not the effect Lofting was looking for.

But one statement in the review is telling—"it shows no lessening in the power and fertility of his [Lofting's] invention." Actually, this novel shows not only no lessening but a great leap forward over the other novels dealt with in this chapter. Here for the first time in five novels is true extended character development, most especially in Tommy Stubbins and John Dolittle himself. There are most unusual plot situations that, though readers of the series had seen their like before, had never been so well crafted and imagined. The Great Sea Snail pales compared with the great lunar moth. There is suspense and startling surprise. There is a sense of unity and purpose in action that gives all the individual adventures a context and meaning. There is no meandering about with a circus wagon here; everything points to the most fantastic voyage of all: the voyage to the moon.

This is not to say that this is a novel without flaws; Lofting never wrote such a thing. The first part of the novel, taking up more than a quarter of the book, comes out of the Home for Crossbred Dogs, which Stubbins, an assistant manager of the zoo, oversees. Quetch, the curator of the Dog Museum, tells the story of his life as he travels around England asserting that he has as much right to live his own life as any human being does. He becomes a gypsy, an acrobat earning his own way, a companion to monks, a sheepdog trainer, and, when he is finally disgusted with human society, a hermit. Eventually he hears of the Doctor and comes to live at his home.

The book really begins with the Doctor's growing interest in insect languages. Having devised a system of hearing the vibrations of insects, Dolittle learns of a race of giant moths. His scientific investigations consume his time, so that he withdraws more and more from the family. To counter this, Stubbins, Bumpo, and the animals inveigle him into a game of blind travel, first introduced in *The Voyages of Doctor Dolittle*. Surprisingly, Bumpo lands a point on a map of the moon, committing the family to travel there. Dolittle has had an inkling that there might be a way of getting there, but he is secretly relieved because he can concentrate on his studies, arguing that the family cannot travel to this place.

But all this is unsettled when a giant moth lands in the garden. Dolittle soon establishes communication with it and discovers it has been sent from the moon in order to bring him back there, though Dolittle is unable to discover why. As Dolittle prepares for his voyage, he hides the moth's presence by keeping it in the back garden, though even then word gets about Puddleby and the curious come to inquire. Dolittle also hides the departure date from Stubbins, though Too-Too has encouraged Stubbins to spy on Dolittle so that he might go along. Dolittle's motive is his concern for Stubbins's safety; Too-Too's motive is his concern that Dolittle should return. But Stubbins has motives of his own: he has not lost the desire for adventure that first led him to Doctor Dolittle, and this alone would be enough to lead him to watch the Doctor closely.

Stubbins eventually disobeys the Doctor for the first time by climbing onto the moth surreptitiously. He reveals himself only after the moth, together with Dolittle, Chee-Chee, and Polynesia, has lifted itself well into the atmosphere. Although at first surprised and possibly even chagrined, Dolittle is actually overjoyed when he finds that Stubbins will accompany him. They cross empty space by breathing into great oxygen-producing lilies and come to hover over the moon, which, in Lofting's imaginative reconstruction, is endowed with an atmosphere. The novel ends as they spy a tree and realize that the moon, in that it has water, can sustain life.

In this latter series of episodes the conflicts of the novels swirl around two human figures: Dolittle and Stubbins. Because he is the narrator, though, Stubbins's conflicts are particularly prominent. The very first word of the book—"I"—is an assertion of Stubbins's presence, and within the first sentence Stubbins will introduce his name, his relationship to Dolittle, his approximate age, and his stance toward the events recorded in *Doctor Dolittle's Garden*. Stubbins's presence will dominate this novel, as it will dominate the next two as well. And the novel will reflect Stubbins's own intuitive growth. It is therefore no accident that this novel stands on the threshold of the more philosophical novels that Lofting would later come to write, for it sets up some of the major philosophical themes of *Doctor Dolittle in the Moon, Doctor Dolittle's Return,* and *Doctor Dolittle and the Secret Lake.*

Stubbins's growth is evidenced in his changing relationship to the Doctor. In introducing himself as the "Assistant Manager of the Zoo," Stubbins is indicating that he is more than merely a secretary; his own skill with animal languages has led to this.[15] He writes that both he and the Doctor "agreed that we must keep a fixed limit on all memberships," while at the same time they together "encouraged development, expansion and new ideas of every kind on the part of the animals" (1–2). Tommy's apprenticeship as a naturalist and his abilities to manage the animals on their own terms—terms exactly like those the Doctor himself worked with—have clearly been established.

This desire to be a naturalist is what leads him to disobey the Doctor and hide on the lunar moth as it begins its flight back to the moon. Stubbins is attracted to the moth just as Dolittle had been. When the moth first appears and Dolittle bids Stubbins to snuff out the candles, "[w]ith trembling hands," Stubbins tells us, "I did as I was told—then sped back to the window and the fascination of this astonishing apparition" (206). Unlike Bumpo, Stubbins is innately attracted to the moth, so that when he later notes that the "animal kingdom held no terrors" for the Doctor (214), he could also be describing himself.

When Dolittle is first considering his journey to the moon, he identifies himself with Columbus pitting himself against all contemporary scientific opinion (259). It is perhaps not surprising, then, that Stubbins too will invoke Columbus as he hovers above the moon's surface (322); almost without recognizing it, Stubbins finds that he is experiencing the exact same feelings that Dolittle himself feels as they are about to land. Stubbins is explicit in terms of what the Doctor feels: awe and thrill at the prospect of discovery, at the utterly strange. But Stubbins's own language shows that this is precisely his own state: "The droning wings of the giant moth suddenly shut off their mighty beating and stiffened out flat, as we began to sail downward towards the surface of this new world which no earthly creature had set foot upon before" (322).

Stubbins is actually wrong in his facts here (he will discover this in *Doctor Dolittle in the Moon*), but his language is suggestive. His use of adjectives, ordering of sense impressions, and dramatic placement of clauses would be quite foreign to the Doctor, but the feelings they suggest are the same as those which Stubbins ascribes to the Doctor. Lofting has here created a character who is almost unconsciously writing about himself. And indeed, the following novels will suggest closer and closer identifications between the two characters.

Stubbins is also beginning to grow in his capacities as a naturalist. He is the one—not Dolittle—who surmises that because the lilies have come from the moon, there must be water there to support them—as well as human life. Stubbins is the one who figures out on which side of the moon they have come down. Yet added to this capacity for scientific investigation is Stubbins's imaginative ability, something Dolittle lacks. While crossing the Dead Belt on the back of the moth, Stubbins recognizes that "the practical Doctor would never bother to remember those things that were not of scientific value to the world" (309). But Stubbins does, for surprisingly his is the larger vision of the meaning of Dolittle's work and life. Over the next three novels, but especially the next two, Stubbins will exercise that imaginative side of his writing more and more, guiding the reader to the meaning of the tales through his own perception. Dolittle will fade as a character in proportion to his own absorption in his scientific work. His retreat from the family circle to his study is emblematic of his retreat from the imaginative world of Stubbins—and the reader.

When Stubbins climbs aboard the moth, he is able to use his imaginative senses to describe the feel of that flight, rather than picture a strictly objective, scientific recording of phenomena. But this is written in tranquillity; what he is more concerned with at the moment is his new relationship with the Doctor: "In everything he had been the leader whose orders were obeyed without question. Here for the first time I had acted on my own in a matter of serious moment and importance. What would happen when he knew?" (299). What does happen is most interesting: Dolittle, for the only time in any of the novels, rebukes Stubbins, though rather haltingly. Stubbins is abashed, wondering if this will be the end of his apprenticeship. And then, in all the glory of restored relationships, Dolittle grasps his arm and tells him, "Just the same, Stubbins, . . . I can't tell you how glad I am to have you with me" (304). He then points out the lights of Oxford and London. Their relationship is most clearly reestablished once Dolittle, from the back of the lunar moth, proclaims that there must be life on the moon. The proclamation comes not to a little boy but to one who in many senses is a partner.

And as the partnership becomes more and more pronounced— as it would be in *Doctor Dolittle in the Moon* and *Doctor Dolittle's Return*—Dolittle withdraws more and more from the worlds he has been used to inhabiting. This, of course, occurs on a literal level: he goes to the moon. But the withdrawal occurs on other levels as well. Increasingly absorbed by his scientific studies, Dolittle will feel the constraints of time. In later novels, after his experience with the long-lived moon creatures, he will generalize these constraints to all humanity. The result is that the Doctor of *Doctor Dolittle's Garden* is no longer the gentle, jovial, portly fellow who is imperturbable. Nor is he the voyager, the man in a caravan, traveling from adventure to adventure. In short, Dolittle begins a process in this novel that is almost unimaginable for the reader of previous novels: he begins to change.

He becomes enormously secretive, quite unlike his behavior in the earlier novels. This secrecy extends even to those closest to him. His work, which had always absorbed him, begins more and more to press against his familial relationships; it is now difficult to get him to sit and listen to a story such as that of Quetch, and the evenings by the fireside when he would tell stories to his animal family are only memories. When the animals try to get him to travel, he responds only very reluctantly; when the blind travel (choosing a destination at random from an atlas) suggests that they must go to the moon, he is relieved to stay home to conduct his study of insect languages. When the animals press him, he responds rather snappishly: "Well . . . I have fulfilled my promise, haven't I? The pencil struck land which no one could reach for the present anyhow. If you'll show me some way I can get to the moon, we'll go. In the meantime—well, we have our work to do" (200).

Still, he is not completely changed. The blind travel had appealed, as Stubbins notes, to the boy in him. And his desire to go to the moon comes about not only because of his desire to investigate it scientifically but also because of his own long-standing love of the extraordinary: "'Stubbins,' he said suddenly in a strange intensive voice, 'if I could get to the Moon! That would be worthwhile! Columbus discovered a new half of our own planet. All alone he did it, pitting his opinion against the rest of the world. It was a great feat. The days of big discovery, as I said, are gone by. But if I could reach the Moon then I could feel I was truly great—a greater explorer than Columbus. The Moon—how beautiful she looks!'" (161) The combination here of intense desire with an interest in scientific discovery is typically Dolittle. But it also connects him to the young Stubbins sitting out on the river-wall and yearning to reach that which seemed so unreachable. These qualities never diminish in Dolittle.

And this is, of course, sharpened as the Doctor begins to realize the rapidity of passing time. In his insect investigations, Dolittle deals with a family of flies called the Ephemera, an apt name, given their short life spans. They live their complete life cycle in 24 hours, and Dolittle musingly compares them to the cycles of humanity, or the much longer cycles of mountains. "But these little fellows," he says, "are content to pack all the joys and experiences of life into twenty-four hours. Some of their philosophy, their observations, should, I think, be very valuable to us" (148). The final pronoun refers not to Dolittle and Stubbins alone but to all of humanity. For Dolittle will find that humanity's cycle differs only in degree, and this thought will press him on during the next novels in the series.

The presence of these concerns makes *Dr. Dolittle's Garden* much more serious in tone than any of the previous novels. The usual light adventures, the frequent comedy from the animals—

such things are missing here. Even those elements which do seem part of the usual fun seem oddly out of place here. The blustering Colonel Bellows, who ran into young Stubbins in the opening of *The Voyages of Doctor Dolittle,* reappears, as do Blackie and Grub from *Doctor Dolittle's Caravan.* But they are mentioned and just drop away. Lofting includes the usual framed tales here from Quetch and from a beetle, but these two are only incidental and disturb the overall tone of the novel. Once the insect languages are introduced and the concern with the moon comes, the book is highly unified and purposeful—and, for the most part, serious.

Doctor Dolittle's Garden brings in three other major concerns that are central to Lofting's thought, though perhaps only tangentially connected to the plot situations of the novel. First, there is a growing interest in the origins of the world—particularly the origins of civilization. Chee-Chee tells an ancient story of Otho Bludge, who was an artist, and his beloved Pippiteepa, who was to become the mother of all fairies. The couple is a rather odd mix of mythologies, but this interest in the beginnings of civilizations will continue in *Doctor Dolittle in the Moon* and especially *Doctor Dolittle and the Secret Lake.*

The second concern is one that has been implicit in all of the novels: the nature of human stewardship over the animal world. When Quetch decides to become a hermit, he notes that "[i]t seemed to me that Man took far more than his share of the good things of this world and that he bossed the rest of creation much more than he has any business to" (66). This is Lofting's voice here just as much as it is Quetch's. Aside from the Doctor and Stubbins, there is only one truly good human steward in all of these novels: Otho. This role will be highly developed in *Doctor Dolittle in the Moon,* though *Doctor Dolittle's Garden* prepares the reader for the development of that role.

The third concern is that of war, and though it is only a minor concern here, it will be of major thematic importance in the next three Dolittle novels. In *Doctor Dolittle's Garden* Lofting is unable to touch deftly on this subject; he hammers at it rather clumsily.

Yet given his background, one wonders if it would be possible for
him to do anything else. Lofting has a wasp named Tangerine
recall a senseless battle that would ravage a valley, a battle that
was one in a long line of attempts to own a valley, as though military might ensured a kind of ownership:

> Yes, indeed, war to us was like a red rag to a bull. It
> seemed such a stupid waste. From either end of our
> beautiful valley armies would come with cannons and
> horses and everything. For hours they would shoot off
> evil-smelling gunpower, blowing some of the trees right
> out of the ground by the roots and destroying simply no
> end of wasps' nests—some of them quite new ones which
> we had spent days and weeks in building. Then, after
> they had fought for hours, they would go away again,
> leaving hundreds of dead men and horses on the ground
> which smelt terribly after a few days—even worse than
> the gunpowder. (109–10)

The senseless passions of humanity are here pitted against the
very sensible, family-oriented, domestic activities of the rational
world of the wasps. The foolishness of the armies is stressed: the
general is named Blohardi; the two armies are the Smithereeni-
ans and the Bombasteronians. The voice here is too moralizing,
too didactic; the power of the piece is lost in its mere silliness. But
the point—that humanity is subject to a kind of meaningless self-
destruction—is made. It will be made more powerfully in later
works.

Christopher Lofting has suggested that by the time of *Doctor
Dolittle's Garden,* this author was growing tired of the character
of Dolittle and wanted to get rid of him by literally banishing him
to the moon.[16] But the evidence of the novel does not agree. None
of the Dolittle novels points toward a sequel more forcefully than
Doctor Dolittle's Garden. The very last lines of the novel, which
include Dolittle's amazed and delightful recognition that water
and life exist on the moon, point toward additional discoveries

and adventures. Having discovered, while hovering just above its surface, that they can live on the moon, Dolittle and Stubbins are on the verge of their most interesting voyage. And Lofting would not leave his readers hovering for long.

The last of the preparatory novels was completed. Lofting then turned to his philosophical works, and Dolittle would never be the same.

4

The Culmination of the Dolittle Series

At the end of *Doctor Dolittle's Garden,* Lofting had left the reader
with Dolittle and Stubbins poised over a new world. In the next
three books of the Dolittle series, Lofting would use the motif of
a new world or a foreign world over and over again. These worlds
would become the settings for Lofting's vision of how a world
should live at peace with itself. And yet the philosophical positions he would take as he established his vision were not new to
the series; the Dolittle family had itself been a microcosm of
a peaceful society, a society able to overcome its instinctive
differences.

The result is that what was implicit in the early Dolittle novels
is explicit in *Doctor Dolittle in the Moon, Doctor Dolittle's Return,*
and *Doctor Dolittle and the Secret Lake.* There is a kind of didacticism that lies not very far below the surface here, but the
strength of these novels is that the didacticism is not overwhelming. Lofting never loses sight of the fact that he is writing a novel,
a fantasy, not a political tract. There is no heavy hand poised to
guide the reader toward political truth. Still, these are novels that
tilt Philip Sidney's definition of literary purpose much further toward the element of delight than that of teaching.

Of *Doctor Dolittle and the Green Canary* and *Doctor Dolittle's*

Puddleby Adventures, it can be observed that it is not necessarily a favor to an author for editors to publish posthumous works.

Doctor Dolittle in the Moon

In 1928 Lofting published *Doctor Dolittle in the Moon*; his readers had had to wait only a year before Stubbins and Dolittle could bound onto the moon's surface. The reviewer for the *New York Times Book Review* was enthusiastic: "[N]ever before has he had quite such astonishing, hair-lifting adventures as he did on this trip, nor discovered such wonders."[1] So. But the reviewer for the *Saturday Review of Literature* was less charitable: "To the present reviewer this latest story of the famous doctor creaks somewhat and runs pretty thin. Most of the illustrations are more careless and uninteresting than former work. The various phenomena furnished by the vegetable life upon the moon rather pall. In fact, we find the story rather tedious. . . . To us the present work is quite insipid cambric tea. It lacks the richness of certain of his former inventions." The reviewer concludes, from the high perch of the royal plural, that "too much good work has gone into some of the earlier books. The present one seems a bit tired."[2] Roger Lancelyn Green would agree: "The invention flags or is too continuously at work: The Doctor's doings on the moon, though cleverly imagined, grow wearisome."[3]

The breakneck speed at which Lofting was writing the Dolittle books would indeed suggest that the novels were becoming tired, but the review for the *Saturday Review,* caught in a sparkling net of metaphors, has misspoken. Elements in the novel show that it is rushed. In three of the illustrations, Dolittle wears his normal suit of clothes even though he had discarded them long ago. Dolittle uses a tuning fork in order to communicate with the Singing Trees, but there is no explanation as to why he has brought something so absurd when he had packed so hastily back on earth. Dolittle and Stubbins wonder whether there is any vegetation on the moon other than a single ancient tree they come upon, yet the

fact that the giant moth brought lilies from the moon should have
answered this question even before they left earth.

But these errors—and the list is not exhausted—characterize a
book that is rushed, not one that is tired. Not since *The Voyages
of Doctor Dolittle* had Lofting been so creative in his setting, so
economical in his handling of tone. *Doctor Dolittle in the Moon* is
actually one of Lofting's most skillfully crafted works, especially
when seen in the context of the entire series. Its ending is as moving as the moment when Tommy Stubbins first sits on the river-
wall and looks out to the horizon.

The novel begins with Stubbins explaining his position as a
writer: he is writing, he claims, to a general audience, and so he
will focus on the wonders and adventures of his trip to the moon;
this is not meant to be a scientific treatise. After remarking that
there was so much to remember about such a strange and novel
place, he begins the actual narrative, having the party—Dolittle,
Stubbins, Chee-Chee, and Polynesia—jump to the moon's surface.
Aside from the moth, the only lunar life they had seen while descending was a large tree, and so they head in its direction. But
having reached it, they still see no additional life.

The tree itself is strange and unworldly; neither Polynesia nor
Chee-Chee will approach it. This uneasiness persists for quite
some time in the novel, as the party feels that there is a kind of
life and consciousness around them with which they are unfamil-
iar. They continue their journey, heading toward a dark patch
Polynesia has spied. Crossing ridge after ridge and virtually overcome by thirst, they arrive at a forest and water; Stubbins faints
with relief.

In the forest and by the shores of a moon lake, their uneasiness
persists. While they continue to sense the consciousness of the
vegetable life around them, they also realize that they are being
watched by the insect and animal worlds, which up to that time
have kept themselves hidden. They discover a huge human foot-
print and recognize that there is more life on the moon than they
had imagined. But soon they make their first contact with lunar
life other than the giant moth when Dolittle learns that the
plants around them are actually speaking; as the plants adjust

their positions to the unvarying wind stream, the sounds they elicit, the scents they send out, and the positions they take are actually forms of communication. Dolittle soon learns the language and is able to speak to the various vegetable communities.

During these conversations the party hears of the Council and its president, but it is clear that this was a slip; the plants were not to have divulged this information. The Dolittle party meets the president, Otho Bludge, a Stone Age artist about whom stories had been handed down from monkey family to monkey family for millennia. Dolittle comes to realize that Otho had been on a part of the earth that had been blown off and had become the moon. He also realizes that everything in the moon is fantastically old, old beyond comprehension. Otho explains how, determined to survive, he learned the language of the animals and plants and created the Council to keep perfect balance between them. There was no death here, or any warfare.

Otho himself is a giant, and indeed everything on the moon is large. Dolittle and Stubbins have also begun to grow and devise makeshift clothing. When Dolittle finds that he has been called to the moon because of his medical skills—many of the creatures are beset by aching parts, and Otho himself has gout—this size presents some difficulty, as the party quickly runs out of medicine and bandages. But they make do, and soon all are ministered to.

When Dolittle determines that he is ready to leave, principally because he is concerned that Stubbins's family will be worried about his disappearance, Otho kidnaps Stubbins, sets him on the back of the giant moth, and sends him back to earth. But when Stubbins is set down on Salisbury Plain, he is nine feet tall. Showing a kind of resourcefulness that Dolittle himself frequently shows, he joins a band of gypsies as a giant and earns enough money to get back to Puddleby, where a normal diet will soon reduce his size.

But when he returns to the animal household without Dolittle, he is abashed that he has left Dolittle behind. The animals reassure him, and they establish a routine life, as Stubbins tries to take the Doctor's place. And each night they watch for a signal from the moon to indicate that Dolittle is returning.

The ending has a subtlety and a many-layered quality about it
that are typical of the novel; like the ending of *Doctor Dolittle's
Garden,* the ending establishes the need for a sequel that will
take up the story precisely where the novel leaves it off. But it
also recalls Stubbins's vigil waiting for Dolittle's return in the beginning of *The Voyages of Doctor Dolittle,* though in *Doctor
Dolittle in the Moon* he is a part of the household rather than set
against it. And it recalls his patient wait on the riverwall, though
now Stubbins is yearning not so much for a place as for a person.
In general, the conclusion is demonstrating Stubbins's growth
and new position in the Dolittle household. Both of those will be
developed in *Doctor Dolittle's Return.*

The complexity of the conclusion is a fitting end to a finely
crafted novel. Despite the catcalls of the *Saturday Review of Literature* reviewer, *Doctor Dolittle in the Moon* is Lofting's tightest,
most focused novel. While the plot situations seem to suggest
multiple tangents that Lofting could have taken, lending themselves in turn to episodic digressions, Lofting restrains himself to
focus instead on the single situation of the party trying to establish lines of communication with lunar life.

But a novel is not well crafted simply because of what an author
has not done. *Doctor Dolittle in the Moon* is also remarkable for
its handling of tone and suspense. Certainly in the context of the
plot everything is strange to the Dolittle party, and so they are
justifiably uneasy. Yet the reader shares in this also, for it seems
at any moment that disaster may come. Until the arrival of the
Moon Man, the tone is unrelentingly ominous. Lofting has written of other similarly strange landscapes, but never has he been
able to sustain this tone and its accompanying suspense for so
long in a single novel. This ominous quality is finally fulfilled
when Stubbins is kidnapped, even though the reader never expects him to be harmed. (There is even some hint that Dolittle
himself knew that Stubbins would be sent back to earth and ar-
ranged the kidnapping.)

Another aspect of finely tuned craft in this novel is Lofting's
ability to give vent to his imagination as he constructs the lunar
landscape without letting the details of that landscape obstruct

plot development; indeed, in many ways the lunar landscape is the story, as Lofting works to unite setting and plot. His physical description of the Vanity Lilies, for example, soon becomes a character vignette, which soon becomes a plot device for introducing Dolittle to many of the vegetable inhabitants of the moon. This leads Dolittle directly to the Whispering Vines, who in turn, though accidentally, lead him to Otho Bludge. All of the elements are tightly held together. There is no meandering here, as in *Doctor Dolittle's Caravan* or *Doctor Dolittle's Zoo*. Even the single frame tale of the novel—Chee-Chee's story of Otho Bludge in the "Days before There Was a Moon"—is incorporated fully into the main plot line.

Doctor Dolittle in the Moon continues some of the interests Lofting had shown in his earlier novels. Like *Doctor Dolittle's Post Office* before it and *Doctor Dolittle and the Secret Lake* after it, this novel is concerned with origins—here, with the origins of the moon. In part this comes in the form of Chee-Chee's legendary stories, but it also comes in Dolittle's dealings with Otho Bludge and in his examination of the chronicle that the lunar community has kept. As with his other dealings with origin stories, Lofting is particularly interested in exploring what went right or what went wrong. In the case of the moon, Lofting depicts a world where things went right because of two qualities: a determination to survive and kindliness: "It was the story of a new world's evolution; of how a man, suddenly transported into space with nothing but what his two hands held at the moment of the catastrophe, had made himself the kindly monarch of a kingdom—a kingdom more wondrous than the wildest imaginings of the mortals he had left behind. . . . And what hardships and terrible difficulties he had overcome in doing it, only we could realize—we, who had come here with advantages and aids which he had never known."[4] It is no accident that those qualities Lofting gives Otho Bludge which enable that character to create a peaceful civilization are those very qualities which Dolittle has been showing all along.

Lofting also continues to focus on Stubbins's growing apprenticeship. As Dolittle and Stubbins spring to the moon, Stubbins

is clearly still in the role of a secretary, a role he retains throughout the novel. But he is also a close companion; he is the one
human being who is truly a friend to Dolittle. For most of the
novel he shares the reactions of Polynesia and Chee-Chee; he is
at times timid, at times dreadfully afraid. But by the end of the
novel he has learned to deal with situations in much the same
way Dolittle has learned to deal with them. When he is kidnapped
and placed on the moth by Otho Bludge, he makes the best of the
situation and prepares for the ardors of the trip home. When he
is left on Salisbury Plain, alone and gigantic, he resourcefully
finds a way to earn money and make his way back to Puddleby.

Once back at the Doctor's home, a very interesting transformation occurs: "And so I settled down to pruning the fruit-trees,
caring for the comfort of the old horse in the stable and generally
trying to take the Doctor's place as best I could" (307). Stubbins
is here fulfilling what had been implied in the previous novel. As
Dolittle withdraws from his animal family—either into his studies or to the moon itself—Stubbins comes to take his place, not as
a usurper but as a companion who fills needed roles. As he had
begun with some of the same qualities as Dolittle, so he gains
additional similar qualities and in fact becomes a kind of heir.

Stubbins is also continuing to develop as a narrator. As with
earlier novels, Stubbins is an older narrator looking back. Only
Polynesia, it would seem, remains of the Dolittle household, and
there is a kind of unstated sadness about the older Stubbins. At
one point he breaks into a eulogy about Chee-Chee, suggesting
that that loss is still vivid, though the actual death of Chee-Chee
is outside of the narrative boundaries of the novels.

The very opening of *Doctor Dolittle in the Moon* is demonstra-
tive of Stubbins's growth in terms of his own conception of himself
and his role as the writer of Dolittle's memoirs:

> In writing the story of our adventures in the Moon I,
> Thomas Stubbins, secretary to John Dolittle, M.D. (and
> son of Jacob Stubbins, the cobbler of Puddleby-in-the-
> Marsh), find myself greatly puzzled. It is not an easy
> task, remembering day by day and hour by hour those

> crowded and exciting weeks. It is true I made many
> notes for the Doctor, books full of them. But that infor-
> mation was nearly all of a highly scientific kind. And I
> feel that I should tell the story here not for the scientist
> so much as for the general reader. And it is in that I am
> perplexed. (1)

The diminutive Tommy has become Thomas, and he identifies
himself first as the secretary of John Dolittle. In *The Voyages of
Doctor Dolittle* he first identifies himself as the son of the village
cobbler; here that linkage is relegated to a parenthetical aside.
He is also reflective about his role as a narrator speaking to a
specific audience. He tries out various approaches with the various animals of the Dolittle household but determines in the end
that he must "set the story down in my own way" (5). This is
precisely what he does, and readers of earlier Dolittle novels will
recognize the reflective style of Stubbins, marked by its leisurely
pace, opening conjunctions linking images and ideas, concentra-
tion on the landscape, and understated tone and meaning.

Except for *The Voyages of Doctor Dolittle, Doctor Dolittle in the
Moon* is the text in which Stubbins is most explicit about his
methodology as an older narrator recalling events in his past. He
is the selective lens through which we see Doctor Dolittle; our
perspective and our knowledge are consistently dependent on his
own. And that perspective is not that of a naturalist. It is instead
that of a writer, of one who is consciously telling a tale and who
sees that telling as the most important part of his endeavor.

This is the reason that several times during the novels, Stubbins insists that, though he has taken volumes of notes on the
natural world for the Doctor, the tales he is telling are drawn not
from those notes but from his memory. He explains his method of
selecting details in his recounting of the first conversation with
the Moon Man: "I will not set down here in detail that first talk
between the Moon Man and the Doctor. It was very long and went
into a great many matters of languages and natural history that
might not be of interest to the general reader. But here and there
in my report of that conversation I may dictate it word for word,

where such a course may seem necessary to give a clear picture
of the ideas exchanged" (229–30). This is precisely his method in
writing the memoirs of the Doctor. For the most part he does not
concentrate on those things which the Doctor wanted to be included in his notebooks. When he does, it is only in terms of their
relationship to the present action. He describes the inside of the
shell of the Great Sea Snail because it is important in their journey back to Puddleby; he explains the nature of moon vegetation
because it relates to the plants' communication with other life on
the moon; he deals with the oxygen-yielding flowers because they
are important in terms of their journey across the Dead Belt.
These explanations are included not for their scientific value but
for their value in terms of the tale Stubbins is telling.

This selectiveness at times leads to a reflexive concern for the
limitations of the writer himself. While on the moon, Stubbins
finds himself "wishing that I were a great poet, or at all events a
great writer" (190). That world is then characterized in a long
sentence whose cadences and rhythms are indeed poetic; it is as
though Stubbins did not recognize his own ability, or perhaps the
images themselves gave rise to a poetic passage: "Trees that sang;
flowers that could see; butterflies and bees that conversed with
one another and with the plants on which they fed, watched over
by a parent council that guarded the interests of great and small,
strong and weak, alike—the whole community presented a world
of peace, goodwill, and happiness which no words of mine could
convey a fair idea of" (190–93). He concludes the passage with
another demurral, though the reader has already recognized that
the order of this world—mirrored in the balanced order of this
sentence—is quite an enviable thing when compared with that of
our world.

And the reader's awareness of the order of that world is something Lofting continually works at—as he would in the next two
novels as well. In this sense *Doctor Dolittle in the Moon* is mor-
alistic and almost didactic, for the peaceful coexistence of the lunar community is meant to serve as a model for earth. Further,
Lofting does not confine the model to humanity; rather, he extends it to include humanity's relationship to the natural world.

Having endowed the lunar plant kingdom with consciousness, Lofting goes on to show how the lack of decay indicates that each tree "looked as though it had stood so and grown in peace for centuries" (54). Later Stubbins notes that "it did seem as though every one of these giant plants that rose about us led a life of peaceful growth, undisturbed by rot, by blight or by disease" (75). When Dolittle compares this to "the struggle for existence" (76) on earth, he expresses scientific curiosity but also longing. The emphasis on peace does not escape him. "Indeed," Stubbins soon afterward writes, "we have found the whole system of life on the moon a singularly peaceful business" (83), given that there seemed to be absolutely no competition between species.

This is contrasted with the foolishness of human struggles, something Lofting had focused on in earlier novels. Chee-Chee tells of a time when the moon first came to be and humanity was divided as to whether or not it should be worshiped. "The war was a terrible one," he relates, "men killing one another in thousands—greatly to the astonishment of the Monkey people. For to us it did not seem that any of the various parties really knew anything for certain about the whole business" (171). Dolittle's sad reply encapsulates his own philosophy of living: "Just as though it mattered to any one what his neighbor believed so long as he himself led a sincere and useful life and was happy!" (171).

The mechanism Lofting establishes in the moon is a Council that assesses the needs of each species and looks out for the welfare of all. The Whispering Vines note that "after the institution of the Council communication and cooperation became much better and continued to grow until it reached its present stage" (188). It has meant, the Vines conclude, the elimination of war. Later, Otho Bludge will make precisely the same observation (237). Dolittle's response is again one of longing:

> "Yes," he repeated, his manner becoming of a sudden deeply serious, "our world that thinks itself so far advanced has not the wisdom, the foresight, Stubbins, which we have seen here. Fighting, fighting, fighting, always fighting!—So it goes on down there with us. . . .

The 'survival of the fittest'! . . . I've spent my whole life
trying to help the animal, the so-called lower, forms of
life. I don't mean I am complaining. Far from it. I've had
a very good time getting in touch with the beasts and
winning their friendship. If I had my life over again I'd
do just the same thing. But often, so often, I have felt
that in the end it was bound to be a losing game. It is
this thing here, this Council of Life—of life adjustment—
that could have saved the day and brought happiness to
all." (189)

Certainly this is not Lofting arguing for the institution of a new
political system to govern human affairs. But it is Lofting point-
ing out that kindness, understanding, and cooperation are pref-
erable to warfare. If this message sounds too overtly didactic, it
is to be remembered that it is couched in the gentle fantasy of Dr.
Dolittle's voyage to the moon, which holds its own intrinsic interest. Yet at the same time, the quality of longing that permeates
this novel and that controls to some extent the imaginative reactions of the characters is a strong unifying element and a factor
in the creation of the moral world that surrounds the character
of Dolittle.

Doctor Dolittle's Return

Five years were to pass before the next Dolittle novel was published, five years that would see tremblings suggesting that the
war spawning the Dolittle novels would not be the only world war
of the century. It was an inordinately long wait, given Lofting's
previous record, and perhaps Christopher Lofting's belief that
Lofting was growing tired of the series after *Doctor Dolittle's Garden* might be more accurately descriptive of his state after *Doctor
Dolittle in the Moon*. In any case, Lofting would never again publish with such rapidity.

Doctor Dolittle's Return was the shortest novel in the series
since *The Story of Doctor Dolittle*; it is about half the length of

some of the other novels. There are fewer illustrations here than had appeared in other Dolittle books, and they are simpler, almost never incorporating any kind of landscape or background. A not-insignificant portion of the book is taken up by references to past novels. Scenes from *The Voyages of Doctor Dolittle, Doctor Dolittle's Zoo, Doctor Dolittle's Caravan,* and *Doctor Dolittle in the Moon* are evoked in the first dozen pages of the text. Scenes from *Doctor Dolittle's Post Office, Doctor Dolittle's Circus,* and *Doctor Dolittle's Garden* follow. It is tempting to suggest that these qualities point to a lack of interest in the story, but given the strong sense at the end of *Doctor Dolittle in the Moon* that a sequel would follow, this seems unlikely.

Certainly *Doctor Dolittle's Return* is less unified than *Doctor Dolittle in the Moon*. The stories of the return from the moon, the reestablishment of the garden community, and the jail are only tangentially connected by Dolittle's concern for writing his book about life on the moon. The framed tale about Dolittle's escape is used with good effect, though, since it is incorporated logically and plausibly within the plot situation. But it is the character development that sparkles in this novel, particularly that of Stubbins.

The novel opens about one year after Stubbins's return from the moon. He has established a kind of routine about the Dolittle house, tending the garden and the animals. He has built an underground library to protect Dolittle's notebooks from fire. He has worked on his animal languages. But what is most important, both for Stubbins and for the animals, is the watch that is kept on the moon, as they all wait for the signal that will herald Dolittle's return.

Stubbins recognizes that because a year has passed, Dolittle will have had time to study all of the moon's seasons. And when he still does not return, Stubbins wonders if Otho Bludge will allow him to leave. Even more disturbing, he wonders if Dolittle wants to leave, given the chance for scientific study and the possibility of greatly prolonged life. But he is distracted by another pressing problem: money. Facing the same difficulty Dolittle had faced before him, he resolves to take a job, and with Matthew's help he secures an accounting position with a butcher, a position that allows him to work at home and watch for the Doctor.

The sign finally comes when the animals are gathered to watch an eclipse, and after a day spent frantically preparing, the animal household waits on the lawn for his arrival. He comes on the back of a giant locust, but the trip is so difficult for him, the air and gravity so strange, that he is unconscious and terribly weak. He is also 18 feet tall, too tall to fit into the house. Stubbins, together with Theodosia and the animals, aligns four mattresses under the old circus tent, and here is where Dolittle sleeps. Meanwhile, Stubbins unpacks all of the specimens that have been brought back from the moon.

One of the "specimens" is a moon cat who had been eager to see the home of her ancestors. Dolittle has reluctantly brought her along, and for a time Stubbins is able to hide her. Soon, however, the other animals of the household discover her presence and are horrified. Even the stalwart and faithful Dab-Dab threatens to fly away. Tommy reminds them all of her pluck and courage in coming to a new world, and eventually, though not without difficulty, she settles into the established household family.

When Dolittle regains his proper size and grows stronger and accustomed to the earth's atmosphere, he sets about a number of projects that recall those of *Doctor Dolittle's Garden*. He establishes a moon museum. He sets the garden to rights. He reorganizes the neighborhoods of *Doctor Dolittle's Zoo*. He rejoins the family circle to tell how Otho Bludge had held him prisoner for a time, and had reluctantly decided to give him the freedom he merited. And Dolittle begins again to see patients.

This last becomes frustrating for him, for he sees that he will always be prevented from working on his book. Matthew Mugg suggests that he go to jail, but Dolittle fears he would be neglecting the animals. When Matthew points out that the animals had been getting along without him while he was in the moon, Dolittle resolves to go. Despite some comic misadventures, he is finally arrested and remains in jail, writing, until he is discovered by mice and rats and badgers, who burrow so many holes under the jail to bring him more food that the structure threatens to collapse.

He returns home dejected, only one-quarter of his book written. But Stubbins assures him that he too has gained considerable veterinary skill. He takes over the duties at the dispensary, having become a true naturalist and skilled animal linguist. Dolittle is left free to write, to pursue experiments with lunar plants, and to speculate on how he might bring longevity and, with it, peace to the human race.

The novel begins and ends with Stubbins looking up toward Dolittle—in the moon or in his study. This is what Stubbins has been doing metaphorically throughout the series, in fact. But in *Doctor Dolittle's Return* Stubbins does more than look up to him; he begins to participate in the kind of life Dolittle had created for himself. This is already clear in the opening paragraph of the novel: "Doctor Dolittle had now been in the moon for a little over a year. During that time I, as his secretary, had been in charge of his household at Puddleby-on-the-Marsh. Of course a boy of my age could not take the great man's place—nobody could, for that matter. But I did my best."[5] There is a kind of reasoned humility here; Stubbins recognizes that he is not Dolittle. But the final sentence of the paragraph suggests that Stubbins recognizes he is able to take over many of the Doctor's responsibilities; by the end of the novel he will take on even more than he has up to this point. This novel is actually a working out of the implications of that opening paragraph.

Stubbins spends much of his time learning and growing as a naturalist, following the footsteps of Dolittle himself. He continues to learn more about animal languages, until the household animals tell him that "it would not be long before I could talk their different tongues as well as John Dolittle, the greatest naturalist of all time. Of course I could not quite believe that; but it encouraged me a lot just the same" (3). His inability to believe his own advances reflects the perspective of a child who cannot believe that he might one day be the peer of his hero. But for the child reader of this novel, that is not hard to imagine.

Stubbins also takes the initiative to set up the underground library. He apparently begins to conduct his own experiments, as Dab-Dab chides him for filling Dolittle's old bedroom with dried plants and specimens. He is the one who sets up the moon museum, earning high praise from Dolittle for his efficiency and orderliness. In short, the early interest Stubbins had shown in animals in *The Voyages of Doctor Dolittle* has matured into a vocation for Stubbins.

At the same time, Stubbins is growing more and more like Dolittle. Part of this is out of necessity, since in this novel Dolittle is either in the moon or in jail. And even once out of jail he is completely caught up in the moon book. It is thus left to Stubbins to manage the household. But this is what he has been doing for the entire novel already. He has managed the financial needs of the family. (When referring to his savings, he notes that "[w]hat I had saved I kept in the same old money box the Doctor used" [32]. The emphasis on the "I" and the reference to past practice is telling.) When the Doctor returns from the moon, it is Tommy who arranges the preparations, who steps out alone to meet him, who establishes his accommodations, who, in short, cares for him. And it is Tommy who sits and chats with the animals, who tells stories by the fireside, who commands, together with Dolittle, the allegiance and love of the animal household. He is the one who saves the day when the animals almost revolt at hearing of the presence of the moon cat. They accept her because of their love for and trust of Tommy, as well as Dolittle.

Most significant in this regard is the growth in Stubbins's veterinary skills. When Dolittle is jailed, the animals who had come for treatment from him find another able hand.

> I got very interested in the work. I felt proud that I could handle sick cases all by myself. Then I began to notice that the line waiting outside the dispensary door wasn't getting any less each morning, as it had at the start. Once in a while a more difficult case would come in, needing pretty ticklish surgery. I wished the Doctor was there to help me. But he wasn't. Some of these were ur-

gent cases that needed attention at once. There was no
one else to handle the work, so I did it. (153)

"So I did it"—this simple assertion might have been spoken by
Dolittle himself. Aided by his skill with animal languages and
Dolittle's own books, Stubbins eventually becomes what he calls
an "assistant doctor" (154). Soon he takes over all the duties in
the dispensary that Dolittle himself had once held. He is well on
his way to becoming a great naturalist in his own right. He is no
longer the young boy sitting on a riverwall.

The emphasis on Stubbins's development overrides the philosophical meanings that Lofting includes in the novel, meanings
and positions that carry on naturally from *Doctor Dolittle in the
Moon*. Recognizing that "any one who studies natural history
must come to fear sooner or later that all life faces a losing game
down here with us" (91), Dolittle resolves to find a way to bring
the peaceful coexistence of the moon to earth. He refers to it as "a
new way of living" (88), and for much of the novel Dolittle works
on how such a new way could be introduced to humanity.

Eventually Dolittle comes to a startling conclusion: that
humanity engages in war not because of self-hatred or a desire to
oppress or sheer acquisitiveness but because humanity is always
pressed for time, rushing about madly to fit everything into a
short life span. On the moon, where creatures live for thousands
of years and may indeed live forever, the impulse toward war is
absent. "That's the thing I'm working for—to bring everlasting
life down to earth," he says. "To bring back peace to Mankind, so
we shall never have to worry again—about Time" (182). Dolittle
too has changed from the early novels, where common decency
and kindness seemed enough to lead to peace. Now he faces something much more basic—and much more difficult to change: the
nature of existence itself.

Stubbins, though he does not pose as an older narrator at the
beginning of the novel, is able to establish some distance between
himself and Dolittle so that he can reflect on the meaning of
Dolittle's concern. Thinking of Itty the moon cat, Stubbins wonders, "[Had] he not perhaps felt after twelve months on the moon

that a year is but a little time in the life of the universe, and that
the moon cat—if and when she would—could still tell him much
he did not know?" (156). Stubbins has here accurately assessed
Dolittle's—and perhaps Lofting's—feelings about the crush of
time. Stubbins himself does not feel it; nor would a child reader.
But for Dolittle it is a dominant concern, tied to his interest in
origins, his interest in Otho Bludge, and his recognition that the
world is infinitely marvelous and worthy of unending exploration.

The result of this concern is a significant change of tone in
these novels. Blishen suggests that "there are shadows, now, over
the Dolittle world, and what for so long was so bubbling and gay
is now shot through with melancholy."[6] And although Lofting is
able to insert the comic into the melancholy—and perhaps these
two are not particularly unrelated—it is hard not to read this melancholy as the tone of a disillusioned author, one who saw that
the world is much as it has always been and is unlikely to change.

Doctor Dolittle and the Secret Lake

When *Doctor Dolittle and the Secret Lake* was published in 1948,
a year after Lofting's death, reviewers greeted it as the last of the
Dolittle books. But with the curious process by which nonliving
authors can continue to produce books, that was not to be: two
more Dolittle books would follow this one. What it would be is the
longest of the Dolittle books, as well as the book with the longest,
most intricate framed tale. Like *Doctor Dolittle and the Green Canary,* the next novel in the series, *Doctor Dolittle and the Secret
Lake* was to be dominated by the framed tale and connected
strongly to an earlier novel—in this case, *Doctor Dolittle's Post
Office.* (Tommy's remark that the window boxes are still being
tended on the old post office houseboat serves to show that
though he had not been here as a character, he, like the reader,
is aware of the Doctor's adventures in Fantippo from the account
in the earlier novel.)

As with *Doctor Dolittle and the Green Canary,* this novel incor-
porates much material that was published serially in the *New*

York Herald Tribune in the early 1920s. Lofting had also incorporated part of the story of Mudface and Noah's flood into the Dolittle series in *Doctor Dolittle's Post Office.* When he died before the book was finished, his wife Josephine finished the editing and concluded the book. It was to prove a happy collaboration.

Reviewers, perhaps for the sake of nostalgia, were very kind to the book. "It is difficult to comment on this last of the Dr. Dolittle books because we keep remembering a child who, a quarter of a century ago, carted the great man's adventures to the tops of apple trees and the far reaches of haymows," reflected the reviewer for the *Atlantic Monthly.*[7] Ellen Lewis Buell, writing for the *New York Times Book Review,* was aware of the deeper implications of Dolittle's character: "Occasionally we agree with Cheapside that Mudface is a bit long-winded, but his story of the start of a new civilization is highly exciting and holds overtones of significance in this post-war world."[8] It does indeed, for this, the last of the true Dolittle series, is Lofting's final word on how humanity ought to govern itself. What is perhaps most remarkable about *Doctor Dolittle and the Secret Lake* is that Lofting's message has not changed, despite the intervention of yet another world war between this and the previous Dolittle novel.

Doctor Dolittle and the Secret Lake opens several years after *Doctor Dolittle's Return*; during those years Dolittle has been experimenting with the seeds he brought back from the moon, trying to find a way to bring the longevity he found on the moon to humanity. But his experiments have not been successful, and as the book opens Dolittle has despaired of success. For the first time he seems to have been defeated in one of his projects, and he is cast into gloom.

Stubbins and Polynesia are determined to help the Doctor out of his poor spirits; as always, the way to do this is through a voyage. When Stubbins suggests that they might try to locate Long Arrow—a strategy he had used before the moon trip—Dolittle, who seems to be something of a defeatist at this point, does not take the bait. But when Stubbins suggests that they might visit Mudface the turtle, who had sailed with Noah during the flood, Dolittle is intrigued. Perhaps the turtle would be able to give him some clues as to the causes of longevity in Noah's time. His desire to go on the voyage is increased when he discovers that the notebooks he had filled with notes about Mudface's life during the last voyage to the Secret Lake have been shredded by rats to make nests. His desire is brought to a height when Cheapside and Becky bring news that an earthquake has buried Mudface and damaged his island. As in *The Voyages of Doctor Dolittle,* the rescue mission becomes the overwhelming impetus for the journey.

And so they set out on the good ship *Albatross* on what was to be Dolittle's luckiest adventure. Everything seems to go just right. A storm petrel warns them about an oncoming storm, which they can then avoid. They make a perfect landfall at Fantippo, where they find that Dolittle's memory is still venerated and the window boxes in the post office houseboat are neatly filled with geraniums. When Cheapside, Polynesia, and Chee-Chee are sent to find Jim the crocodile, they come across him almost immediately. He in turn is able to convince millions of crocodiles to swim to the Secret Lake to free Mudface.

By the time Dolittle and Stubbins arrive, this task has been almost completed. When it is finished and Mudface is freed, troops of monkeys set up a small village for the Dolittle party and the crocodiles repair the damaged island. Mudface then begins the long history of the flood, which takes up the second half of the book. The setting is appropriate, for beneath this lake lies the remains of Shalba, the city where Noah lived and worked as a zookeeper.

Mudface begins his tale with recriminations for Mashtu, the king of Shalba, who imprisoned him as well as Eber, a slave who was made to assist Noah. Eber's kindness wins Mudface's approval, and when the rains come and Mudface, along with his wife, Belinda, scampers upon the ark, his only regret is that Eber has not been saved as well. When the rains have finally ceased and all the world is flooded, Mudface happens to look out and sees Eber, together with Gaza, a beautiful slave whom Eber loved, floating on an uprooted tree. When Noah refuses to help the pair, Mudface and Belinda leave the ark and carry the two to a floating house. Mudface searches in the drowned cities for food and wine in sealed containers, and, provided with these, Eber and Gaza survive. Eventually they find dry land, build a hut, and begin a garden.

But once the waters have gone down, the animals released from the ark find them. Determined that humanity shall never again enslave them, the animals decide to kill Eber and Gaza. But Mudface and Belinda convince them that the only way the earth will be reseeded is by the efforts of human beings, and so the grass-eaters stand against the meat-eaters. Eber and Gaza are enslaved by the animals and made to replant the earth.

But the meat-eaters revolt; Eber and Gaza escape into a bog with the help of the two turtles. After a long and difficult journey through drowned, eerie jungles, they reach a newly created sea. The group builds a rude raft and, guided by a raven, crosses the Atlantic and begins life anew on the coast of Brazil. After the birth of a child to the couple, signaling that humanity will go on, the two turtles reluctantly return to the Secret Lake, and there they continue to live.

Before the Dolittle party leaves, Mudface tours them through Mashtu's palace. There they find his accumulated treasures, which Dolittle leaves because of the spilled blood they represent. The only thing he takes along is a bronze crown, a cheap thing Mashtu had had made in order to mock the last people he had not subdued. When they had been defeated, he had planned to be crowned king of all the world. But he had never subdued them; the flood had intervened. And so, laden with the crown, Dolittle, Stubbins, and the rest of the members of the animal household return to Puddleby-on-the-Marsh.

With the possible exception of *Doctor Dolittle in the Moon,* this is the best written of the Dolittle novels since *The Voyages of Doctor Dolittle.* It shows Lofting's typical delight in the strange, the unusual, and the exotic; the Secret Lake and the sunken city of Shalba are as perfect a setting for adventure as the moon or the floating island; it is set apart from and against the ordinary world of Puddleby-on-the-Marsh. The novel also shows again Lofting's interest in stories about origins. As in *Doctor Dolittle in the Moon,* Lofting has Dolittle question how things came to be the way they are. And if *Doctor Dolittle and the Secret Lake* is not particularly interesting for its character development or its narrator, it is nonetheless a worthy addition to the Dolittle series for the sheer inventiveness and fascination of the story itself.

Doctor Dolittle and the Secret Lake is divided into two halves, which is understandable, given the way the book was written, wherein a body of previously published work was incorporated into the Dolittle format. Mudface's narrative begins on page 180, almost the exact middle of the novel. But it is not an easy uniting, for the two halves of the novel are radically different in terms of their concerns. Though it seems as if Mudface's narrative will carry on the concern of longevity—this is, in fact, one of the major reasons for Dolittle's voyage—actually that narrative ignores longevity and moves to completely different concerns. In that sense the book is not successful; its success as a novel depends on the inventiveness of its plot situations rather than its unity. Still, that is true of almost all of the Dolittle novels.

Stubbins is the dominant narrator only of the first half of the novel; once Mudface begins, Stubbins's brief accounts of the listeners are only interruptions. The opening of the novel reflects the fact that Stubbins is writing not as the older narrator crafting Dolittle's memoirs (a role he had assumed in some of the early novels) but as a writer keeping track of events more or less as they happened (the stance he had assumed in *Doctor Dolittle's Return*). "I was writing at my office-table, in Doctor Dolittle's house; and it was about nine o'clock in the morning," begins the narrative.[9] Though put in the past tense, a specificity and an immediacy exist here that do not suggest the style of a memoir.

The change in narrative stance is significant, for it means that the narrator has no chance to reflect on the meaning of events, something Stubbins had always been able to do. The very immediacy of the events negates the possibility that they might be seen within a larger context. Now perhaps this is not a major difficulty, since so much of the novel is taken up by another character, but Stubbins as a narrator seems too preoccupied with scribbling down notes and being awed by the African landscape to have any acute awareness of the implications of Mudface's story. When he paddles off with Dolittle, he is chastened not by Mudface's tale but simply by the fact of having met someone so unutterably old. The result is that for the first and last time in the Dolittle series, Tommy is a naive narrator.

Nevertheless, the narrative style remains typically Stubbins. When the Dolittle party first puts to sea, Stubbins describes the ship in a way that is reminiscent of his prose in *The Voyages of Doctor Dolittle*:

> Of course our sloop was small. The weather was only what regular sailors would call a swell. But I liked the way our boat handled it, the way she rode over the crests of the waves and down into the troughs between. There was something about the brave little *Albatross* (buried out of sight, she was half the time) which gave you confidence and trust in her. The morning sun glistened on her bright new paint; she moved like something truly alive; and the tang of the salt spray on your lips made you glad to be alive with her, in this wide world of water where she seemed so much at home. (101)

Here Stubbins has endowed the *Albatross* with life by evoking sensory images, and he has linked his own sensory impressions to the movement of the ship, establishing a close relationship between character and setting. And like a child narrator, Stubbins must at times resort to cliché to express his sentiments, but the clichés are endowed with such energy and childlike enthusiasm that they are not allowed to fall flat.

As a character Stubbins has grown from the time of *Doctor Dolittle's Return*. He now has a regular office—the old waiting room the Doctor had used before he worked with animals. He is quite comfortable with the responsibilities for the animal clinic given to him at the end of *Doctor Dolittle's Return*. He speaks animal languages almost as well as Dolittle, and certainly, Mudface assures him, better than Noah. He is still the secretary but no longer the apprentice.

Dolittle himself continues the process of withdrawal from the life of the animal household that he had begun in *Doctor Dolittle's Garden* and really worked at in *Doctor Dolittle's Return*. At the beginning of *Doctor Dolittle and the Secret Lake* he disappears from the household so that he might have a chance to think clearly. His studies absorb him to the point that he is almost unaware of others around him; where before his studies had infected others with his own enthusiasm, now they isolate the Doctor. And so the animal household is not particularly displeased when he determines to give up the studies on longevity. Nevertheless, even the termination of these studies does not lead to Dolittle's rejoining the family. He is isolated now by the gloom of failure.

This is a very different Dolittle from the character in the early novels. Where before he had always been the one to initiate action, now he is acted upon. Determined to raise his spirits, Polynesia and Stubbins plot strategies behind his back. While Cheapside goes to find news of Mudface, Polynesia warns against Dolittle's becoming involved in another project too soon; she and Stubbins are determined that they should go on a voyage. "Now, what I want you to do," says Polynesia, "is to try your best to side-track the Doctor from getting started on any new important work before Cheapside pays us another visit" (57). And so Tommy goes about doing this.

And in some measure he succeeds. Dolittle will eventually even rejoin the fireside gatherings he had once frequented. But the thing that will eventually free him from the gloom and isolation of his studies and their failure will be the call to an act of kindness: he will recognize that if Mudface is to be freed from the island that has toppled upon him, he must travel to the Secret Lake. This, more than his scientific studies, is what propels him. This act of kindness will be repaid by Mudface's narrative history. It is the first example of kindness repaid in this novel, and it anticipates a theme of the second half.

The great concern of the first half of *Doctor Dolittle and the Secret Lake* is the theme of time, a theme reflected by the long life of Mudface and Belinda in the second half. Articulated at the end of *Doctor Dolittle's Return,* the concern is for how humanity's brief life allows for no peace. Dolittle's assumption is that if humanity can be given long life and thus be freed from the pressures of time, humanity will then be at peace. It is an assumption that is never questioned in the series, and certainly Dolittle himself never questions it. The failure of his own experiments are therefore a loss of his own precious time and the loss of his dreams for benefiting humanity.

By implication, however, the second half of the novel does speak to Dolittle's assumption. Mudface has had a tremendously long life, but he has not consequently been freed from distress. His story is a tale of great tribulation, during which he must battle the foolishness of men and animals. In later life he is beset by problems from the natural world: an earthquake buries him. It seems clear that the kind of peace for which Dolittle is searching does not come simply through an extension of time. The tremendous irony is that the narrative suggests that it comes through a quality that Dolittle has possessed all along: kindness. And this is the subject of the second half of the novel.

Mudface is the narrator of the second half, and it is, of course, reasonable that someone of his great age would not be particularly concerned with the passage of time; nor would he be inclined to reflect, like Dolittle, on the relationship of time to human peace. As a narrator Mudface is principally concerned with plot and character; he is not the reflective kind of narrator that Stubbins can be. And in so doing he explores, both consciously and unconsciously, the merits of kindness.

Now all through the Dolittle books Lofting is concerned with human kindness; this is one of the central character traits of Dolittle. But nowhere is Lofting more explicit in his insistence that the basis of right relationships is kindness, and that kindness will be rewarded. It is a lesson as old as the oldest folktale, and in *Doctor Dolittle and the Secret Lake* two examples dominate. The first is Dolittle himself, who travels to Africa to rescue Mudface. When the great turtle is freed and rises above the water to meet Dolittle, his greeting is telling: "Again, John Dolittle, you come in time of danger, in time of trouble—as you have always done. For this, the creatures of the land, the water, and the air shall remember your name when other men, called great, shall be forgotten" (173). Dolittle shall be rewarded in a very tangible way: he will hear and be able to read the story of the flood. But he is also rewarded by a kind of legacy that transcends petty human pretensions at greatness. Dolittle will be remembered as a great man because he will be remembered as a kind man: "And thus, as old Mudface himself had said, the creatures of the wild remembered John Dolittle and his kind deeds; they tried in every way to repay him" (177).

Noah and Eber, as characters in Mudface's story, also stand as examples of kindness. Both are kind to the animals; despite the fact that they are treated cruelly as slaves, they are able to treat others with compassion. As such, they stand in direct contrast to Mashtu, the king of Shalba, whose response to those around him is to enslave. In direct response to Eber's kindness, Mudface and Belinda rescue him and Gaza and contrive to guard them against perils, from both the landscape and other animals. As Dolittle leaves Africa, he murmurs, "Good-bye Mudface! . . . Who knows how much you changed the history of the world—in gratitude for the kindness of one man, Eber" (362). In the context of this plot, the effect has been immeasurable.

This kindness by the turtles comes about despite humanity's seemingly inherent bent toward cruelty. When the other animals warn the turtles that someday humanity will rise to enslave them again, the turtles recognize that they are quite right. But that recognition does not negate the acts of kindness that bind one individual to another. Or, to put it another way, Mudface does not allow the pressures of a group, of the past, of instincts, of bias, or of immediate need to dissuade him from the moral obligation owed to one who has shown him genuine kindness. He, as one who has been enslaved by a man, has every reason to take vengeance upon the race. But he does not.

Mudface himself is very conscious of this lesson, of this need for kindness, and of the possibility that kindness will bring a general peace. As Dolittle prepares to leave, Mudface tells him that the publication of this story may end war and help to prevent the rise of rulers like Mashtu. But Dolittle—and Lofting, who had lived through two world wars—is not hopeful: "For men are deaf, mind you, Mudface—deaf when they do not wish to hear and to remember—and deafest of all when their close danger is ended with a short peace, and they want to believe that war will not come back" (360). This is Lofting intruding into the narrative; a reader hardly expects Dolittle to make such a speech. But it is the culmination of a sentiment that is intrinsic to the entire novel.

This concern with human kindness might have been anticipated in this late Dolittle novel. What could not have been anticipated, however, is the religious quality Mudface connects to his acts of kindness. As he tries to prevent Eber and Gaza from being eaten, he claims that the flood was not simply an amoral event coming out of chaotic and random natural forces:

> "Do you suppose this Flood was an accident, like stubbing your foot against a stone? No. Some One—I don't know Who—but Some One planned all this. The King of Shalba made himself ruler of almost all the world. But his rule was bad. . . . [T]hen this Some One, whose name we do not know, but whose greater power controlled the rains, the tides and the fires in the sleeping volcanoes, made up His mind that the world and its so-called civilization must start again from the bottom of the ladder" (269).

Mudface concludes with a sobering claim: "It was not planned that Man should pass from the Earth—not in this Deluge anyhow" (270). This is the first passage of this kind in all of the Dolittle novels, and though it may be inherent in the myth of Noah's flood, it is striking to find this claim in the mouth of Mudface. The implication is that civilization foundered because it was not built on kindness, which is a moral norm established by, according to Mudface, "Some One." It is a moral norm that is violated by Mashtu, with disastrous consequences. One can hardly help but read this as Lofting's allegorical comment on the world wars of his century.

Mudface will later suggest to Belinda that they were appointed by this "Some One" to protect humanity and help it to begin to flourish again (340). Belinda agrees, and consequently they feel a kind of parental love and responsibility for Eber and Gaza—and their descendants. When word comes to them that war is being fought and that even those in America are participating (here Belinda is referring to World War II), she journeys across the Atlantic to be sure the descendants of Eber and Gaza are safe. Lofting does not tell us what she finds.

This religiosity is somewhat problematic. The difficulty comes in that the entire series is built around comedy, fantasy, and even at times broad burlesque. Here the story takes on a poetic and religious quality that is completely alien to the rest of the series and even to the first half of this novel. Where before Lofting had been able to include serious material within the comic format, here he abandons that format to try his hand at something quite different. In the words of Blishen, "the building grew a little higher than its foundations could bear."[10]

At the end of the novel Dolittle is no longer preoccupied with time; he is slightly cynical about the possibilities of real peace. But he has had one thing affirmed: that even in the absence of time and peace, kindness is a dominant virtue. And so he and Stubbins head back home: "Then, like one man with one thought, John Dolittle and I plunged our paddles into the starlit waters at the same moment" (366). It is as if they have at this moment become equals, and Stubbins's long apprenticeship is over. In the context of Mudface's story and moral affirmation, they become one. Here is the true conclusion to the Dolittle series, the true culmination of all the concerns Lofting had been working on since *The Story of Doctor Dolittle.*

Doctor Dolittle and the Green Canary

In 1924 Lofting had written the story of Pippinella, the green canary, to appear in serial form in the *New York Herald Tribune*; he had later condensed some of that material to use in *Doctor Dolittle's Caravan*. That was an uneasy marriage, but it worked at least in part because Pippinella's biography was only a portion of the larger narrative. By contrast, in *Doctor Dolittle and the Green Canary* the material from the serial publication dominates the book, so that Pippinella's life takes up the first three-fifths of the novel; the last section deals with further adventures of the green canary in association with Doctor Dolittle.

Lofting had written most of the material for the book and drawn the illustrations in the mid-1920s, and he had always intended to publish it as a separate book. Prevented by Lofting's death, the book seemed as though it might languish. Olga Ficker, Lofting's sister-in-law, had, however, helped him compile the stories of Pippinella, and she offered to complete the text. This she did, at least in part by adding an opening chapter as well as a concluding one. The book was published three years after Lofting's death.

It is always a dangerous thing to conclude another author's work, or to organize or edit a work after an author' death. One can hardly imagine that Hemingway would have been glad of the publication of *Islands in the Stream,* or Steinbeck of his *The Acts of King Arthur and His Noble Knights,* or Charles Dickens of the various "completed" editions of *The Mystery of Edwin Drood* (with the possible exception of Leon Garfield's, wherein the two narratives are seamless). It is very difficult to completely assimilate an author's stance, to replicate the language, to finish a plot so that it is consistent with the approach the author has shown through the body of his or her work.

Fricker is not especially successful at overcoming these problems. The opening chapter is too bald a summary. The bits of Pippinella's dialogue seem to fit in only oddly, and the quickened, almost breathless summary rushes the reader through material that has already been seen in *Doctor Dolittle's Caravan.* Now certainly it is not problematic to orient a reader, but if a novel is to work—even a novel in a series—it must be able to stand alone. None of the other novels in the series—not even *Doctor Dolittle's Return,* which depends so much on the readers' knowledge of *Doctor Dolittle in the Moon*—opens this way. Almost all of that opening could be cut with little loss.

The final chapter is also problematic. The concluding chase scene works quite well, and since Lofting had illustrated that scene it must be assumed that that was his conception. But the rest of the chapter is, again, too quick, too bald. Everything is wrapped up too tidily, too speedily. And there are problems in the plot situations. When the thief is finally caught, he begins to confess to Dolittle, but actually nothing prompts this: for all the thief knows, Dolittle may have been one of the other two men who had come to steal the papers earlier. The thief then recognizes Dolittle's companion as the one who owns the papers: "If I'd 'a' knowed this bloke were the rightful owner I'd 'a' been 'appy to turn them over to 'im."[11] But, in fact, there is no way he could have known that this bloke was the rightful owner, never having seen him before. And even the quick decision to go back to Puddleby is different from any other ending in the series; it is made quickly and decisively, whereas the whole series had pointed to the fact that though this was the kind of decision Dolittle would like to have made, in fact he was consistently prevented from doing so. And then there is the problem that bluejays have spread a rumor that Dolittle will return, though nothing in the text suggests a motive for such a rumor.

It is hard to imagine that a child reader would not have been disappointed by this novel; Dolittle is so conspicuously absent for so long. But reviewers were generally kind. Writing in the *New York Times Book Review*, Ellen Lewis Buell, who had always been kind to Dolittle works, wrote seemingly rejoicing in the fact that another Dolittle novel simply existed: "There is, indeed, more suspense than nonsense, but the basic humor, the kindliness, the ingenious imagination which are the hallmarks of the Dolittle tales are all here."[12] It would not have been amiss of her to point out that most of this novel is not a Dolittle tale at all.

The novel begins around the time of *Doctor Dolittle's Caravan*, when Dolittle first found Pippinella. After a brief expository section on Dolittle's circus adventures, Pippinella tells her life story. As is evident rather quickly, she has traveled widely. Owned for a time by the manager of an inn, she becomes renowned for her songs and her cheerful greetings to those who frequent the inn.

She is eventually purchased by an imperious marquis, of whom the innkeeper is afraid, and is given to his wife. Pippinella brings some of the few happy moments in that woman's life, for she recognizes that her husband brutally oppresses those who work in the country. Eventually the workers rise against him, killing him and setting the castle ablaze. Pippinella is saved from the fire by one of the soldiers who have come to rescue the marquis, who sees her cage hanging outside a castle tower.

And so she begins a career as a company mascot, for it is believed that she has good luck and is a survivor. For a time she lives with the soldiers, but when they are ordered to bombard a group of workingmen and allow themselves to be captured instead, she is taken as spoils of war and eventually won in a raffle by a miner. He takes her to a new town, and she begins her life underground, sniffing the air for deadly gas. Purchased from the mines by Aunt Rosie, she finds a comfortable home until she is given to a window cleaner, whom she learns to love, despite their poverty.

This man is actually a writer working to overthrow an oppressive government in another country, and he is separated from Pippinella when he is kidnapped by agents of that country. Pippinella is freed and becomes a wild bird; disappointed in love, she determines to cross the Atlantic and search for a new home. She lands on Ebony Island and finds happiness for a time, but soon she misses the window cleaner. Determined to find him, she flies aboard a steamer heading back to Europe; when another castaway is brought on board, she recognizes her master, who has escaped from his kidnappers. Together they return to try to find the papers he had used to write his book; however, while they are trying to break into their former residence Pippinella is stolen by a tramp, who sells her to a pet store. It is from this store that she is rescued by Dolittle.

Dolittle, Jip, and Pippinella begin to search for the window cleaner, and with the help of Cheapside they locate him in a London hospital; he is delirious over the fact that his papers have been stolen. They return to the mill where he had lived and find that indeed agents of the country he has attacked have attempted to steal those papers, but now they are being held by a tramp who senses their value. After a long chase, the tramp is finally run to ground by Jip and a pack of dogs, the papers are secured, and Dolittle determines to return home to Puddleby.

Some elements of this narrative are very familiar. The long narrative accompanied by a related set of adventures involving Dolittle recalls the structure of *Doctor Dolittle and the Secret Lake*. The story of the faithful animal's search for a kind master recalls almost exactly the story of the Prison Rat and his artist master in *Doctor Dolittle's Zoo*. And there is the usual interplay between the various members of the animal household, as well as a series of adventures in which Dolittle is aided by his knowledge of the animal world.

But there are significant problems in the novel as well. Almost all of the framed tale has been told before, and though much is fleshed out, much is familiar. At times Lofting or Fricker will insert skimpy summaries, almost as though to remind the reader that the novel cannot stand on its own. Not until page 173 does the book break new ground, beginning at the point that *Doctor Dolittle's Caravan* concludes. From here on, as Buell notes, Lofting does use suspense to drive the narrative along, and these pages are engaging for their sheer plot. They do not, however, have the kind of depth that a reflective narrator like Tommy Stubbins can give them.

A second problem, though, is the—there is no other word for this—clumsy effort to integrate the story of Pippinella with the story of Dolittle. Mostly this is done by periodically breaking into Pippinella's narrative to include lines from the animal household. Repeatedly, each of the animals is given one line to speak (there is little true interaction) and then Dolittle silences the group so that Pippinella can go on. There is hardly any true dialogue between the animals and Pippinella. (Perhaps the one exception is Gub-Gub's repeated cry to find out what happened to the window cleaner and his comic frustration when the answer is consistently delayed.) There is no integrated whole here, no feeling of true unity, as there is in *Doctor Dolittle and the Secret Lake*.

Perhaps the most interesting element in this novel is a tension that lies beneath the surface of its plot structures: the tension between human cruelty and oppression and human kindness—a tension Lofting developed explicitly in other novels. Human cruelty is manifested most clearly in war. A pigeon speaking to a rather naive Pippinella describes war as "a messy, stupid business. . . . Two sides wave flags and beat drums and shoot one another dead. . . . [I]t never seemed to me that anyone, not even the generals knew any more of what it was all about than I did" (14).

But if war is simple foolishness, there is also a kind of malicious oppression shown in this novel. On a large scale it is shown by governments that, when attacked because they deal unjustly with their people, react with further injustice—in terms of the plot situation in the novel, they kidnap the window cleaner. On a smaller scale the oppression is shown by characters like the Marquis, who control absolutely people's economic lives and who therefore see people as machines, to be replaced when they are no longer cost-effective. The Marquis is attacked because of an attitude: for him, it is irrelevant that he has idled workers and created starving families; he is making a profit.

The result is a set of living conditions that is destructive of the soul:

> "The first impression that I got of the town as we approached it was anything but encouraging. As I have said, there had been no rioting here and work was proceeding as usual. For more than a mile outside all the grass and trees seemed sort of sick and dirty. The sky over the town was murky with smoke from the tall chimneys and foundries and factories. In every spare piece of ground, instead of a statue or a fountain or a garden, there was a messy pile of cinders, scrap iron, junk or furnace slag. I wondered why men did this; it did not seem to me that all the coal and all the steel in the world was worth it—ruining the landscape in this way.

And they didn't seem any happier for it. I looked at
their faces as we passed them, trudging down the streets
to work in the early morning. Their clothes were all black
and sooty, their faces pale and cheerless. They carried
little tin boxes in their hands which contained their
lunches, to be eaten in the mines or at the factory
benches. (52)

Lofting makes no overt didactic statement here, but the collection
of images—sick trees, murky air, furnace slag, dispirited people—
combine to create a vivid impression of despondency created by a
kind of economic despair. This is not to say that Lofting approves
of the actions of the miners—actions that would have analogues
in the British social history of the time—but the images suggest
an understanding of what leads to despair and violence. Like Pippinella, these families are caught in cages and subject to the
whims of masters.

Opposed to those images of almost meaningless oppression are
contrasting images of purpose. Pippinella sees her lot as a hard
one in the mine, but she is also filled with a sense of purpose: she
is protecting those men who work beneath her. An image of song,
color, and life in dreadful circumstances, she rejoices that she participates in human affairs: "I felt something was being done, ac-
complished, as each loaded wagon rattled past my cage on its way
to the hoisting shaft. And I was helping, doing my share" (57).
This is not Lofting mouthing the banal sentiment that one should
try to be happy no matter what the circumstances; instead, he is
suggesting that work should have purpose and meaning and
value.

Connected to this is the need for liberty. While in the mine,
Pippinella longs for freedom, even though she recognizes the inherent dangers a wild bird faces. She contrasts liberty not to a
caged life but to a life filled with sameness, filled with unending
and mindless repetition. And though Pippinella is occasionally
reminded that a cage may afford security and comfort—she is especially reminded of this when she sees a cat with a bird in its
mouth—she will still end the book as a free bird who has con-

sciously chosen loyalty to one she loves. She stays with her master and comes back to his shoulder because she chooses to, not because he forces her to return.

The novel is also filled with images of kindness. An anonymous passenger gives money to the window cleaner on board ship. Aunt Rosie rescues Pippinella from the mine, as the soldier had rescued her from the burned tower. Dolittle resolves not to return to Puddleby until he can find the missing papers, and when Dab-Dab chides him for this, Jip replies, "Listen to who's talking, Doctor. Why, Dab-Dab spends every minute of every day doing something for others" (224). The window cleaner writes his book because, as Dolittle notes, "[i]f someone doesn't do something about the unfortunate people in other countries they may soon start another war—and then, sooner or later we'd get mixed up in it, too" (257). Those images are the normative ones, those Lofting weaves into his narrative as a kind of balance to the images of oppression that fill Pippinella's tale.

At one point during the story of her life, Pippinella tells Dolittle, "You know a canary is a somewhat smaller creature than a human being, but his life and what happens in it are just as important for him" (59). Here is Dolittle's philosophy reduced to its basic core; here is the principle by which Dolittle lives. And, one feels, if there is a single message calling out from the Dolittle books, this is it.

Doctor Dolittle's Puddleby Adventures

Doctor Dolittle's Puddleby Adventures was the last of the Dolittle books to be published, and though some greeted its arrival with glee, a modern reader might be less enthusiastic. Jane Cobb, writing for the *New York Times Book Review,* began her review by asserting that "the regret with which Lippincott announces that *Doctor Dolittle's Puddleby Adventures* will be the last of the series is an emotion that will be shared by many of us."[13] Perhaps. But in many ways this is the least interesting of the Dolittle books, perhaps because it is the one in which Lofting himself is distinctly absent as an organizing artist who creates unity, wholeness, and integrity out of seeming randomness.

Doctor Dolittle's Puddleby Adventures—a misnomer, since most of the adventures neither involve Doctor Dolittle nor occur in Puddleby—is a loose grouping of stories already published in the *New York Herald Tribune* during the 1920s. The result is that although they resemble the framed tales of the Dolittle series, they in fact lack the framing that gives the stories purpose and sometimes even meaning in the earlier novels. There is no internal unity; indeed, an obvious kind of unity is overlooked. As is mentioned again in this novel, Dolittle and Stubbins had begun collecting animal biographies from the Rat and Mouse Club. Here Dolittle suggests doing the same thing for the Home for Cross-Bred Dogs. The first half of the book contains stories from within this context, and so the idea of animal biography could have organized an entire collection. As it stands, however, everything seems random. It is hard to believe that Lofting would have applauded this volume.

The early sections—at times just the first paragraph—of the stories were written by Olga Fricker, and these, though they sometimes seem repetitive, work well. Not only do they establish a context for the stories, but they also introduce the narrator—often Stubbins—and set a tone. Generally there is a seamless flow from Fricker's text to Lofting's, something that was not present in *Doctor Dolittle and the Green Canary.*

In the foreword Josephine Lofting claims that this collection contains "some of the best of my husband's works."[14] This hardly seems true. The various episodes often lack the kind of wit, suspense, internal consistency, and purpose of other tales. Many of the adventures seem gratuitous and random. In the maggot's story, a nest that is his friend's home is picked up by a sailor, brought to his bunk area, dropped, picked up by rats and brought outside, dropped and picked up by another sailor, brought back to the bunk area, dropped, and . . . well, there it is.

If the stories can be connected, it might be through adventure and travel, two elements that characterize all of the tales. The Sea Dog tells of his adventures aboard the *Sea Swallow,* as he is shipwrecked and befriended by a cabin boy. The Sea Dog is eventually responsible for the boy's rescue, after they have been separated—gratuitously—some three or four times. Dapple, the thoroughbred, tells of his misfortunes under the handling of a wealthy owner, until he escapes to the Home for Cross-Bred Dogs by pretending to be mixed. Stubbins relates the tale of comic misadventure dealing with the dog ambulance, whose first patient is Gub-Gub.

The other stories are more haphazard. "The Stunned Man" tells of a mare who escapes the oppression of its groom. "The Crested Screamers," told by Cheapside, shows how those birds rescued him from an owl. "The Green Breasted Martins" shows Dolittle rescuing birds that were being killed in Africa because of a new fashion. "The Story of a Maggot," identified in the foreword as one of Lofting's favorite stories, deals with the adventurous life of the seafaring maggot mentioned earlier in this discussion. And "The Lost Boy" is a comic tale of a mischievous boy's antics at Dolittle's Circus. None of these have the kind of compelling suspense that fills many of the stories in earlier volumes, and this suggests that Lofting might have substantially rewritten some of these tales had they been included in a novel.

Many of the pieces collected in *Doctor Dolittle's Puddleby Adventures* are strongly connected to specific Dolittle books; in fact, they have the feel of pieces edited out of those books owing to a lack of space. This gives them a sense of authenticity, as though they had been conceived of as part of a whole, so that the connection to a novel is not merely whimsical. The opening half of the book might just as easily have appeared in *Doctor Dolittle's Zoo* as the stories of the various rats and mice. The story of the crested screamers, which is connected to the Canary Opera, and the story of the lost boy might have appeared in *Doctor Dolittle's Caravan*. And the story of the green-breasted martins might easily have appeared in *The Story of Doctor Dolittle* or even *The Voyages of Doctor Dolittle*. If one wishes to press this even further, the story of the maggot—the only story not distinctly connected to one of the earlier novels—might have been attached to *Doctor Dolittle's Garden,* given Dolittle's interest here in insect languages. A reader beginning the series with this book will make none of these specific connections, but one familiar with the series will certainly make them and thus have a context for these tales. Without such a context, they can hardly help but appear random and haphazard.

Olga Fricker's introduction to the book asserts that Tommy Stubbins is the author of all these tales. And though at times he is awkwardly introduced into the stories, he is a very real presence, both as a character and as the narrator. Because these are early stories, he has lost much of the stature he had gained by *Doctor Dolittle and the Secret Lake*; here he is very much the young boy. But the implication behind Fricker's comment is intriguing, for it suggests that Stubbins is the author and narrator of even those adventures in which he did not take part; here, this would include the story of the green-breasted martins, which occurred after Dolittle's adventures in Jolliginki. The narrative stance of this story—and of the non-Stubbins books—is so different from those in which Stubbins is the narrator as to make this suggestion suspect, however.

Like so many of the Dolittle novels, this collection is difficult to characterize in terms of a unifying theme. It would be better to define the stories in this collection as having a consistent focus, one that extends back to the first novel in the series. Lofting is always suggesting implicitly and asserting explicitly that each animal's life is significant to itself. To recognize that is to recognize the legitimacy of a relationship between humanity and the natural world that is truly stewardly and not mechanistic or even authoritarian. When the maggot suggests that all creatures are deserving of respect, Dolittle agrees: "This idea of . . . revulsion and dislike on the part of one member of the animal kingdom for another is quite baseless and stupid" (172). Now the effect of this statement is somewhat mitigated by the fact that Dolittle is here speaking to a maggot (one would be hard-pressed to find something quite so loathsome to the Western imagination), but the sense is consistent throughout the Dolittle books.

At the beginning of his adventures, another maggot suggests that all creatures are faced with certain limitations and that all creatures are called to overcome them. This equalizing and leveling of the animal kingdom is part of the focus, part of the emphasis on the integrity of each individual. The strength of the Dolittle novels is that while Lofting was maintaining this somewhat didactic focus, he was also sustaining the gentle wit and imaginative play of the plot situations. Perhaps the resolution of this possible tension is Lofting's greatest narrative accomplishment.

5

The Minor Works:
The Elements of Nonsense

Hugh Lofting's legacy to children's literature is clearly his Doctor Dolittle series; today his minor works are virtually unknown. Certainly they are completely unknown to almost every child reader. Of the eight minor works he composed, all but *The Twilight of Magic* have long been out of print—justifiably, in most cases. And yet there is the odd moment in some of these books where Lofting's deft hand is at work in creating a nonsense world that is filled with imaginative life.

Edward Blishen suggests that Lofting should be accorded a kind of minor status in the history of nonsense verse, and surely his *Porridge Poetry* must be placed in the tradition of Edward Lear and Lewis Carroll, though it would be hard to imagine a convincing argument that would put him in their company.[1] But this is Lofting's poetic tradition, and his inclination toward it is of a piece with all of his work, which has a nonsense list to it.

In nonsense the world is turned upside down as the reader's perceptions are skewed, as all that might be expected is cheerfully undercut and actually reversed, so that a table and chair will stroll through town, or a pussycat will marry an elegant fowl. The meaning of nonsense literature comes through the reader's awareness that reality and perception are being played with and manipulated in new ways. And so animals can suddenly talk to human beings, and pigs can write books.

Gub-Gub's Book

Lofting wrote two books tangentially connected to the Dolittle series: *Gub-Gub's Book* (1932) and *Doctor Dolittle's Birthday Book* (1936). Of these, *Gub-Gub's Book* is the one to most fully participate in the nonsense genre. Ostensibly the book is a history of food, and the book is portentiously framed with end papers depicting a world map indicating where certain foods are to be found. The seriousness of the maps is subverted by the corpulent presence of Gub-Gub himself, posed as a learned writer. The book, as the title indicates, is meant to be Gub-Gub's, and from his perspective it is a book of high seriousness. For the reader, the book will be a skewing of history and folklore toward an emphasis on food, Gub-Gub's chief interest. It is this skewing that provides much of the book's humor.

The novels in the Dolittle series include a number of references to Gub-Gub's proposed 20-volume history of food. (As the title page indicates, this has been reduced to a single volume: "Owing to the High Cost of Living the other 19 Volumes of this GREAT WORK have been Temporarily Postponed.")[2] Ostensibly, this volume is the working out of Gub-Gub's intention. In fact, though, throughout the book Lofting makes strong connections to the Dolittle series, and although the good Doctor himself never appears, his presence is invoked repeatedly. The animals of the Dolittle household do appear, however, and references are made to earlier episodes, such as the Puddleby Pantomime, in which Gub-Gub played a prominent part. The result is that readers familiar with the series are able to place this book within a context; without that context, the book is an odd amalgam of odd stories that has no internal unity or even purpose.

The book is divided into 10 evenings by the fireside, during which time the animals listen to the stories of Gub-Gub. The

Dolittle books contain frequent references to these kinds of evenings, and the animals yearn for them once the Doctor no longer has the time to attend. Typically the stories are framed and interrupted by a good deal of banter and some bickering between the animals, but it is clear that as the 10 evenings progress, the animals are more and more entertained by Gub-Gub's nonsense stories. Thus while he is often ridiculed and set against the rest of the animal household—as he is in the Dolittle series—Gub-Gub is also recognized as a storyteller.

Each of the evenings is a compilation of anecdotes Gub-Gub has gathered from his research. He tells of the wars between the yellow and red tomatoes, the case of the raja's missing eggs, the story of Quince Blossom and the military uses to which her dreadful cooking was put, the saga of the king of the Grand Picnic. These tales in turn call up short tales from the other household animals, all of which are in some manner connected to food and cooking.

Stubbins is the narrator of this book, and the opening chapter is his discussion of how he came to work on it. His stance is typically Stubbins: "Yet for whatever faults this book may have, Gub-Gub must not be held entirely to blame. Perhaps I am by no means the best person for the work. Maybe I am not what is called a good editor, that is, one who is clever at arranging, and putting in good understandable words, the writings and sayings of others. But at the time that this was written there were very few people, besides the Doctor and me, who could understand animal languages" (14). The almost posed humility is typical of Stubbins. Even the fact that he has taken on the task is typically Stubbins, since he has done it so that Gub-Gub will not take up the Doctor's time. One irony here is that Stubbins has shown before that he is actually quite good at editing a collection of materials. Later Stubbins notes that in the construction of this book "I had sorted out from the great mass of his [Gub-Gub's] writings those parts which I thought people—human readers—would like best" (18). This is precisely the method Stubbins has used all along in editing the great mass of Dolittle's material: selecting, putting passage and incident within a context, and preparing it all for the general reader. Stubbins is once again the selective lens Lofting has established.

This very selectivity is one of the sources of the book's humor. Although ostensibly this is Gub-Gub's book—his history of food, as the title page proclaims—Stubbins's method has undercut Gub-Gub's authority, an authority that is constantly questioned by the household animals. The authority is further questioned by the very form of the book, which is not so much a history of food as a narrative history of the household's stories about food, told around a fire. Similarly, Gub-Gub's role as an artist is subverted when Stubbins suggests that his mud illustrations could not be reproduced in a book. Stubbins himself then becomes the illustrator of the book, though under the pig's supervision. But here even Stubbins's authority is subverted when a reader comes to the illustrations and finds that they are signed, rather prominently, not by Stubbins but by Hugh Lofting. Subversion upon subversion, the result is that only a small portion of this book is actually by Gub-Gub. And therein lies the humor.

The form of this book is suggestive of the *Tales of the Arabian Nights,* which are divided into a series of nights in which stories are recounted. In fact, this is much the same format Lofting employs, as the animals entertain themselves with story after story. It is perhaps for this reason—to establish the context of a gathering of storytellers—that Lofting has the animals invoke many familiar tales, all slanted to emphasize some quality of food. The folktale of the stone soup is retold, references are made to nursery tales ("Miss Muffet and the Curds and Whey" [65]), the stories of Shakespeare and Aesop are recalled, Sherlock Holmes is renamed Sherbert Scones to fit into the theme, and stories of Robin Hood, Captain Kidd, and Troy are mentioned. The result is a strange hybrid of a book, filled with a miscellany of tales all tenuously connected by the ways in which they touch on culinary matters.

As with his other books, Lofting does compose some somber notes into the work. Once again he pictures war as an enterprise to be despised because it is meaningless and, in the end, non-

sense. When a country is divided by civil war over the question of
whether one should eat red or yellow tomatoes, Gub-Gub notes
that the country has gone to the dogs. "The dogs would not have
taken such a silly country as a gift" (61), replies Jip tellingly, suggesting the foolishness of humanity. An opposing image is set by
the king of Guzzledom, whose story is the longest in the book.
When his country fights over a similarly meaningless question,
he announces that "[w]hatever happens, there shall be no war. I
spent my days teaching the people what are the good things of
Life and Peace: shall I end my days by shooting them like dogs?"
(154). Here is one of the few wise rulers in a Lofting book, and
though the king is deposed for a time, his view is the one that
triumphs.

The values this king holds to are the values Dolittle himself has
held to: domesticity, the worth of each individual, joy in the simple and gentle things of life, an acceptance of the circumstances
of life. These are the values celebrated in a sonnet Gub-Gub
translates earlier in the text:

> Reposefully awaited in this house of mine,
>   The knowledge of the value of these things,
> Shall make the Coming of Life's End,
>   Instead of something dark and grim
> The pleasant Visit of a Gracious Friend. (138)

When Gub-Gub recites this, Stubbins notes that the animals are
"oddly solemn" (137). They are indeed, though they may not recognize it at the moment, hearing a philosophy of life that Dolittle
espouses, and that Lofting himself espoused.

But *Gub-Gub's Book* was not meant to be a philosophical work.
When Dab-Dab hears of the pig's plan to write a book, she chides,
"It is too bad . . . that you can't find something useful to do with
your time" (48). But Whitey's response is different: "It must be
rather fun to write a book" (48). It is the fun and delight in nonsense that is at the heart of *Gub-Gub's Book,* and while the volume is not remembered today, it is a work of interest to those

familiar with the Dolittle series and as an example—minor
though it may be—of the nonsense genre as applied to children's
literature.

Doctor Dolittle's Birthday Book

In 1936 Frederick Stokes published *Doctor Dolittle's Birthday
Book,* a small, squarish date book. It was one of several of the
minor books that would be published in a small size. Since it came
out well into the Dolittle series (nine Dolittle books preceded it),
it was clearly marketed for the young readers who had become
loyal to the series. Each two-page spread featured four dates followed by short quotations, mostly from the character of Dolittle:
"Don't be downhearted," from 3 January, or "Now that I'm living
in a postoffice, I can't think of a single person to write to," from 6
January.[3] For the most part the quotations are humorous and
evocative of Dolittle's character.

The dated pages are preceded by a five-page account of Puddleby birthdays narrated by Stubbins. If the book is significant
at all—and outside the context of the Dolittle series it is not—it
is for these pages. In dealing with life in Puddleby, Stubbins
evokes certain aspects of Dolittle's character that are familiar to
all readers of the series. For example, Dolittle advocates buying
presents for someone whenever he sees something appropriate,
whether or not it is that person's birthday. It is a generous gesture
but an impractical one, as he cannot restrain himself; Dab-Dab
helps by hiding a gift until the appropriate holiday.

Similarly, Dolittle's artistry is evoked when Stubbins recalls
the plays, pantomimes, and dramatic comedies Dolittle wrote for
various animals. And the Doctor's sensitivity and kindness are
suggested as he orchestrates various celebrations to make them
appropriate to the animal: Gub-Gub's party is held in the kitchen
garden; Too-Too's midnight picnic is held in the woods. But the
most prominent feature of Dolittle's character that emerges is his
childlikeness, seen especially with Dolittle's delight in fireworks

and with a punch bowl-circus. When Matthew Mugg remarks that Dolittle will never grow old, Dab-Dab replies tellingly, "Never grow old! Sometimes I think he'll never grow up" (ix). It is this whimsical and gentle look at the Doctor's character that gives this small book its significance.

Porridge Poetry

Porridge Poetry, published in 1924, represented one of Lofting's two sustained efforts at poetry. This book collected a group of comic nonsense poems in a hand-size volume; the format set a single poem against a single illustration, many of which were colored plates. The title of the book, marked by a humorous alliteration, suggests that this book, like *Gub-Gub's Book,* could be characterized by an emphasis on food. Even the title page announces that this is a book "cooked, ornamented, and served up by Hugh Lofting."[4] In fact, however, there is no consistent theme, or unity of any kind.

The reason for the disparate nature of the collected poems may lie in the vision of the collector as Lofting imagines him. The opening poem is entitled "The Porridge Poet," and the image Lofting pictures, in both the text and the accompanying illustration, is of a poet who mixes together ingredients into unusual combinations:

> Shake in an ounce of sifted syntax
> And half a teaspoon of tin tacks,
> Then flavour with eggstravaganza,
> And there you have a lovely stanza! (11)

Leaving aside the question of literary skill for a moment, one is struck by the odd juxtapositions, the curious mess of the stanza. It is this that marks the entire collection: an unexpected and unpredictable mixture of very different poems.

"The Porridge Poet" as a title is also suggestive of the audience to which Lofting is appealing. This is meant to be light, comic verse: "And as for comic songs or ballads / I turn them out like summer salads" (8). The poet is identified as cook, combining ingredients in delightful ways. And as if to further subvert any sense that the poetry here collected is in any way formal, Lofting chooses a rhyme scheme that does not scan perfectly; each line seems to end with an extra unaccented syllable:

> My verse is very free and easy,
> Its flavour sometimes slightly cheesy;
> But that, my friends, is no great crime in
> The gentle art of kitchen rhymin'. (7)

In the third line the final unaccented syllable in what seemingly should be a line of iambic pentameter is especially troublesome; it carries great weight because it sets up the rhyme for the next line. Yet that fourth line seems to end with something of a cheat, as the poet cuts the word to manipulate and force the rhyme. The result is a loose, informal poetry, not the free verse of later decades but a verse that stays within conventional boundaries—barely. Poetry here has become a delightful concoction.

At times the freedom of Lofting's verses is problematic. "Vera Virginia" is something of a scansion nightmare:

> Oh, what a popular person I am!
> My full name is Vera Virginia Ham.
> The barn-dance, the two-step, the sausage-roll trot,
> The pig-jig, the hog-jog, I dance the whole lot. (12)

Anapests dominate the first two lines, though the opening of each line is irregular and the first line, even with the addition of the superfluous "Oh," is a syllable short. The next two lines will end with anapests, but the rest of the lines will be dominated by spondees divided by two unaccented syllables and an iamb. Perhaps the chaotic rhythm is meant to replicate the various dance rhythms that are mentioned, thus comically undercutting the pretentiousness of the speaker, who is, after all, only a pig. But it may be that this is simply bad art.

Dance rhythms are especially suggested when "Vera Virginia" is juxtaposed with the following poem, "The Lollipopinjay." Here too the speaker is performing a dance:

> For I'm the lollipopinjay.
> I loll by night, I dance all day.
> I jump, I crouch and pop away.
> Skip! Hop!—Tip-top! Hip, hip hooray! (14)

The iambic meter of the first three lines is very regular, and this, combined with the short words and short phrases, simulates a dance step. The fourth line is all the more striking because of the regularity of the first three. The three opening spondees, like a change in step, slow the reader down, while the closing iamb ties this line back to the first three. The rhythm of each foot is thus perfectly suited to its role.

The apparent freedom—or laxity—of the poem is more of a problem in "Scallywag and Gollywog":

> Scally Wag and Golly Wog
> Took their bag aboard a log
>   And started off to cross the ocean blue.
> They're still at sea, I have no doubt,
> For all they do is fight about
>   Which shall be the Captain, which the crew. (124)

While this poem presents a delightful image and its rhyme scheme suggests a kind of tightness, the poem's rhythm is distinctly off. The line lengths are so established as to imply a prearranged form that structured the poem without any reference to its meaning. The first tercet opens with two seven-syllable trochaic lines and concludes with a line of iambic pentameter. The second tercet shifts to eight-syllable iambic lines followed by a nine-syllable line dominated by weak verbs and pronouns. This is poor art not because a poet must necessarily be consistent in a rhythmic pattern but because shifts in rhythmic patterns must come of necessity. The shift must be suggested by the text at the same time that it gives the text meaning. This is most certainly not the case here.

One other problem that the Porridge Poet's laxity leads to is a sometimes careless juxtaposition of ingredients. In "The Porridge Poet" the poet mixes "sifted syntax" with "tin tacks." It is hard to escape the sense that the latter was chosen simply because of the dual rhyme. And while that is very musical, the image is jarring in a poem that has focused exclusively on poetry and cooking; the rhyme is not enough to make this an appropriate image in the text. When in the following two lines "eggstravaganza" is paired with "stanza," one can hardly help feeling the heavy hand of a poet whose rhymes are not inevitable but forced.

But all this is not to suggest that there is no merit in these poems. Above all, the nonsense context of the poems allows Lofting to revel in sounds and relationships between sounds. "Ella, fella / Maple tree / Hilda, build a / Fire for me," begins "Picnic" (20). A boy crying over a broken toy is called a "grubby, snubby, tubby, chubby, scrubby little boy" (30), the nonsense words given meaning by the true words. "Oom-pah, boom-pah, oom-pah, boom!" (32) sounds a brass band, the sounds and rhythms reproducing the effect of the illustrated trombone and tuba. And barber chimpanzees chant "Clippety, snippety, clippety, clop!" (70). The chief delight in each of these poems lies in their repeated sounds.

At times this delight in sound will mix with a certain playfulness with language:

> 'Twas in the tropic latitudes
> That we were talking platitudes,
> Just sailor-like chit-chatitudes,
>   As any ship-mates might.
>
> We forgot to take our longitude
> (Which was a grievous wrongitude)
> So we didn't reach Hong-Kongitude
>   Till very late that night. (16)

The delight here is not only from sound but from the formulation of nonsense words by following the patterns of real words. The opening syllables of those words each rhyme, connecting the first three lines of each stanza. In addition, the final lines of each stanza are connected by their end rhyme. It is a tightly packaged poem that works because of its playfulness with language.

Much of the imagery Lofting uses is highly evocative. In "The Palm Family" a group of palms under a silent yellow moon lives free from harm: "And when the wind blew soft and low / They'd whisper tales of long ago" (26). The image is a fertile one, full of potential, its peaceful visual image mirrored by a slow rhythm and the assonance of "soft," "low," "long," and "ago." But here Lofting does what he often does in this collection: stop too soon. Having set the image, he drops it and moves to a new poem. One wonders what stories of long ago might be to a palm tree. Lofting is content to let the reader wonder.

This is an oft-repeated pattern. A seaside seagull resolves to abandon the oceans: "I'll go ashore and settle down / In some peaceful country town / And wear my carpet-slippers when I drink my china tea" (66). But this is the end of the poem; the richly evocative image is dropped. Similarly, when the Household Drudge turns her back on a china basin of fudge, "the poodle dipped his face in!" (88). But the—one might suppose—interesting reaction of the Drudge is never evoked. And while at times it seems that the poet is purposefully restraining himself to allow the reader to finish the poem, at other times there is a distinct sense that the poems, most of which have only eight lines or fewer, are simply not fully developed. One need only compare "The Rat and the Guitar" with Edward Lear's "The Owl and the Pussycat"—on which the Lofting poem is based—or "Betwixt and Between" with Lewis Carroll's "Tweedledum and Tweedledee" to get a sense of Lofting's less-than-full development:

> Betwixt and Between were two
>   betwins,
> Their father's name was Twoodle.
> They've been alike as a pair of pins
> Since they could scarcely toddle. (82)

It is the rhyme scheme alone that gives this poem any interest, for the implications of the twinness are not worked out.

Not insignificant in this volume are the illustrations by Lofting. While in most cases these are merely decorative, at times they contribute to a poem's meaning. The illustration for "Oom-Pah" (33) identifies the brass band as the source of the poem's sound. That for "Vera Virginia" (13) adds the audience she is ostensibly addressing. The fullest union of text and illustration comes in "Jim Nast of Pawtucket," whose protagonist slides down the stairs in a bucket: "He has more understanding / Since reaching the landing. / Just look at the hole where he struck it!" (68). Here the poet directs the reader's eye to the accompanying illustration, which depicts a hole down which Jim Nast has presumably disappeared.

In the end *Porridge Poetry* has to be defined as a minor work in the genre of nonsense poetry; it is even to be considered a minor work within the writings of Lofting himself. Its power comes from its play with sound and its sometimes delightful images: a seagull sipping "china tea" (66), a dog who is "loose in the middle" (56), two pigs on a "milk-and-honey honeymoon" (74), the "pirate of the kitchen sink" (36). These nonsense images, while not the most powerful images of his work, attest to Lofting's whimsical imagination.

It is tempting to look in minor works for connections to an author's major works. To do so here is to invite disappointment. And yet one poem suggests a major concern of the later Dolittle books. In "Wei Hai Wo" the mandarin sage sits at his window, watching the scurrying life of those in the city and singing, "How silly, Lily, lackaday! / Deary daisy me!" (43). When he is reproved by his friend, he replies,

> If others wish to run about
> Then let them. But let me look out.
> I've found that peace, my good Sin Ching,
> Is quite the most important thing.
> You see now why I sit and sing. (47)

Dolittle too will come to this conclusion, though his route to it will be quite different. In a collection of nonsense poems this one stands out as qualitatively different. It is not so much the work of the Porridge Poet as of the author of the Dolittle novels.

Victory for the Slain

On 18 June 1940, Winston Churchill stood before the British House of Commons and delivered what may be his most memorable speech. Only the day before, France had fallen; Britain now stood virtually alone against Hitler. "If we can stand up to him, all Europe may be free and the life of the world may move forward into broad, sunlit uplands," Churchill intoned, preparing for his final line, a line that would move a nation and make it want to be brave just for its prime minister: "Let us therefore brace ourselves to our duties and so bear ourselves that, if the British Empire and its Commonwealth last for a thousand years, men will still say, 'This was their finest hour.'"[5] It was a not-insubstantial rhetorical barrier erected against the storm.

But Churchill's was not the only British voice raised; nor was his the sole vision of what the war was about. Published in 1942, in the middle of the war, Lofting's reflective poem *Victory for the Slain* represented a different voice. Written during the height of the Blitz, it questioned the entire enterprise of war and saw no possibility of grandeur in it. For Lofting, war could never be a "finest hour," but only one disastrous moment in a succession of disastrous moments: "None but the criminal can be made / To plunge into a heart he was not taught to hate / A bayonet's cold unthinking blade."[6] And so, for Lofting, "In war the only victors are the slain" (10).

The tone of this, Lofting's single adult work, is unrelentingly ominous and grim. The narrator is frustrated by peacetime apathy, the martial ardor of the youth, the recurrency of wars to end all wars, the blind folly that leads to such destruction as the fire-bombing of Coventry Cathedral. The narrator—and, one suspects, Lofting as well—is disillusioned, plagued by memories of

World War I's horrors, despairing, a heir of Gertrude Stein's lost generation in a sense and yet not, for one solace is left: his faith. But even this is only an uneasy solace, for the church in which he escapes from the urgency of today reminds him again and again of war:

> Your columns of columns march unending—
> Processional stone,
> Phalanxed and symmetric, wending,
> Adeste!—Sing!" (10)

Here the sense of a religious procession moving up an aisle merges with the procession of sweating infantrymen that open the poem.

There is a different kind of nonsense at work here:

> Must Mankind forever kill and kill,
> Thwarting every decent dictate
>   of the human will?
> War again!—
> When well we know
>   War's final victors always were the slain. (28)

This is the nonsense of repeated folly, the folly of failing to learn from the past. It is a theme Lofting touched on in the Dolittle novels, but here the grim tone barely holds back an anger at humanity. It is not a work of children's literature, and almost as if to emphasize that fact, Lofting chose a publisher other than Stokes to print this book.

In the poem the narrator ascends High Street toward the cathedral, passing "khakied squads of infantry" (5) and a maimed veteran of World War I as he goes, emblems of the omnipresence of war in his country. As he moves into the church, he begins a long meditation on human folly and unwisdom, inspired by the various structures and objects he sees around him: the poor box, the baptismal font, the tombs, the chancel. While it seems that each will lead to a kind of comfort, he finds that in fact the comfort of the church's structure is illusory. "The walls are strong. / The roof is frail" (15), the narrator notes, the combined short sentences dramatically suggesting the narrator's own instability.

And, in fact, at the end of the poem the bombs do come, ripping through the roof and destroying the altar. The narrator's final hope is evidenced in his prayer, in his dedication to the church though it may lie in ruins, and in his commitment to the slain— his absolute insistence that humanity will move into a better way and validate the hope for the statued saints that lie so still and hopeful within the cathedral.

The cathedral itself is unnamed, though Lofting does at first seem to suggest a particular site, given that he names two prominent Saxon kings who are buried there: Aethelstan and Aethelred. In fact, however, these two are buried in different places, Aethelred at Simborne in County Dorset, Aethelstan at Malmsburg Abbey at Chippenham. The implication is that Lofting is invoking names rather than establishing a particular site; this could be any church, any cathedral, up any of the innumerable High Streets of England. (At the same time, Lofting's use of those two Saxon Kings fits well with his theme of recurring war, for the reigns of both were marked by long battles against the Danes, Aethelred perhaps dying from wounds incurred during a battle. Even Malmsburg Abbey is appropriate, in that it was pillaged and burned by the Danes in the eleventh century. Today only ruins remain.)

The seven-part structure of the poem corresponds to seven progressions by the narrator. He begins with a journey upward, past infantry (which he leaves behind) and a maimed veteran (whom he also leaves behind) to seek the solace of the church (which he will not find). What he will find is a mixture of beatitude, recurring memory, and delusion: "There!—Was that a flash / I saw through incense-mist? / A gleam!—A naked sword?" (11). This leads to the second movement, focusing on the poor box and engendering a proclamation on the destructive power of the drive to wealth: "Money—power in the Past, as now, / Make continents in devastation burn" (13).

In the third movement the narrator enters farther into the church, walking down the aisle under which are interred the remains of Saxon abbots. This brings on a musing about death, and curiously the narrator feels no fear. "Give me your hand again, as once you did / In Flanders, such a little time ago" (17), the narrator asks, speaking directly to death as he recalls his own World War I experience. He concludes that "Life itself is but your twin in hope" (19) as he looks about him at the marbled sepulchers and sees the dead resting in peace. Even Chatelaine lies peacefully, a carved spaniel at her feet, despite the death of her husband on a crusade and his burial far away. Addressing her, the narrator concludes that "This peace, for which in life you sought, / To us, in after-life, you taught" (21).

The chancel, that area which will be destroyed by the end of the poem, is the setting for the next three sections of the poem. As the heart of the activity of the church is centered at the chancel, so are these sections the heart of the poem. Driven closer to absolute despair by the recognition that war seems to be an unalterable and recurrent entity within human history, the narrator is saved by the very solidity of the structure he sees about him: "My Sanctuary, / My Sanctuary in stone!" (26). But even this is not a compelling hope, for the narrator suggests that humanity is degenerating:

> Perhaps, Omnipotence, long, long ago
>   You touched our hearts
> With exaltation's lifting glow,
> To kindle growth we never guessed—
> To pull us through Dark Ages' guilt—
> And thus this psalm in stone we built;
>   But later slowly changed,
> Unknowing that we cast away
> Our tranquil stature day by day;
> Till back to littleness we crept,
>   Where, in oblivion, our visions slept.
> And now,
> We look at *this* and wonder how
>   From hands like ours it ever came.
> (27)

Opposed to this vision the narrator places modern science, which he dubs blind, something without vision. The grim irony of the comparison is that science will destroy the thing of vision at the poem's end. Still, the narrator calls on the Allied forces not to respond in kind as they invade Italy and march toward Rome, not to "court the stigma of the 'V' / For Vandals" (32).

The poem's final section begins in the Lady-Chapel, a place of quiet prayer. Here occurs the poet's prayer to the Madonna: "Hold staunch and fast / This only shield for us, the Shield of Peace / That shall not pass away" (35). But it seems to be a failed prayer, for as he leaves, the bombers come and part of the chancel is destroyed. The narrator himself is driven to hatred, railing against the "foul vultures of the night" (37), having lost the tranquillity he had found in the Lady-Chapel and even descending into a kind of lost hopelessness: "Where are you walls?—The dark! / My sight—my day is gone" (38). The poem concludes with a resolution to learn the lessons of the past, and to find the meaning of the victorious slain and, in so finding, preserve that meaning.

The principal theme of the poem is familiar to a reader of the Dolittle novels: the meaninglessness and folly of war. And yet despite its folly, it is constantly repeated. Even the walls of the church whisper a millennium of requiems for those who died in foreign wars (9). The two world wars are "fits" that "return / And cause . . . / All building of the centuries to burn" (23). And so Lofting's narrator rejects the drive for power and wealth that leads to war, the apathy of peacetime that does not lead to the preservation of peace, the military jingoism that enraptures youth and sends it to fields like Flanders, and even the Victorian imperialism that had marked Lofting's own youth:

> Is it not equally to blame
> To teach God's children, "My Country, right or wrong";
> "The White Man's Burden"—or that "Right is
>   Might"—
> Or that to dominion by conquest
> For evermore they should proclaim
> The dedication of their very race's name? (16).

Opposed to the drives toward war, Lofting juxtaposes the image of the maimed veteran, the "[p]oor, listless soldier, maimed, / Bravely trying to re-design / A shattered life / With but a single hand" (29). It is a disturbing juxtaposition, one that would never appear in a Dolittle novel, and one that contributes to the narrator's despair.

Part of that despair comes about as the narrator recognizes the relationship between the past, present, and future. At the beginning of the poem the narrator comes to the church "[t]o refuge from the Now and Present" (6), and even as he enters "[t]he blatant noises of To-day / In murmurs mould and melt away . . . / Mellowed into Past, reborn, / Now change to bygone, more melodious strains" (8). It is the present the narrator attacks; insisting on itself, it ignores the lessons of the past and the prophetic calls of the future. The result is the "futile frenzy of recurrent War" (23). It is only in the chancel, which Lofting defines as a bridging of the past and future over the "querulous Present" (22), that the narrator finds any real relief from the tensions of the immediate, tensions that Dolittle himself, in quite another context, is not unaware of.

Perhaps the largest irony of the poem is an unresolved tension that the narrator himself seems unaware of: the tension between dealing with the exigencies of the present even as one denies the primacy of the present. In more concrete terms, there is the Nazi war machine to be dealt with even as one laments humanity's inability to live in peace. Unable to escape this tension, the narrator can only hope that the victorious slain shall one day lead humanity to an enlightened peace. The note of resolution at the poem's end refutes the despair that characterizes the rest of the poem. And in refuting that despair, the poet rescues the refrain "In war the only victors are the slain" from becoming merely grim; in the end the slain become victors because they offer hope through lessons, a hope emblemed by the recurring image of the small, half-opened cathedral door that, though "swayed by the force of World's wild winds" (29), will stand ajar though the "[s]torm is brooding on your lintel yet" (38). It is a modest hope, but a hope nonetheless.

Certainly this is not a great literary effort, but it suggests Lofting's own struggle against despair. The Dolittle book that followed this poem—*Doctor Dolittle and the Secret Lake*—would also hint at despair in its awareness of the persistence of humanity's folly. But it too would hope for peace and for bright virtues that would overcome the frenzied fits of a world at war with itself.

The Story of Mrs. Tubbs

The Story of Mrs. Tubbs is a slight tale, written in 1923, during the great rush of books in the early years of the Dolittle series. Like several of Lofting's books, this was printed in a hand-size volume with rather large printing on alternate pages—a format expressly designed to appeal to the young child. In general, most of the illustrations are cruder than those of the Dolittle novels, though this volume includes more color than is used in any of the Dolittle books.

The title is reminiscent of the first Dolittle novel and, like that novel's title, is used to introduce a folktale quality into the story. Everything that happens in the short tale has a folktale feel to it: the advanced age of Mrs. Tubbs, the black-and-white characterization, the three-part structure of the story, the domesticity of the ending. The language Lofting employs also emphasizes this quality: "Once upon a time, many, many years ago, there lived a very old woman and her name was Mrs. Tubbs. She lived on a little farm, way off in the country. Her little house stood on the edge of the woods, not very far from a village with a little church, and a little river with a little bridge over it, flowed close by the house."[7] The formulaic opening, matched by the equally formulaic concluding line, sets the story within the folktale genre and prepares the reader for the acceptance of certain folktale conventions. The tale is set long ago, emphasized by the repetition of the adjective *many*. Mrs. Tubbs is unimaginably old; later it is suggested that she is more than a century old. She lives on the edge of a wood—an archetypal setting—and not far from an idealized village. Before the plot situation even begins, the narrator has established its parameters.

The story itself is archetypal: the expulsion from and search for a home. Turned out by the landlord from the farm she had inhabited for many years, Mrs. Tubbs sets out with her dog, duck, and pig into the countryside. She is replaced in the farm by the landlord's red-faced nephew, dubbed Beefsteak-and-Onions by the dog. Having no place to go, Mrs. Tubbs sits under a tree and sobs. From this early moment on, she is inactive; the animals take responsibility for her welfare. (In that sense they are not unlike the Dolittle animal household.) They find a cave, catch and cook some food, and gather leaves to warm her as she sleeps.

The next morning the animals begin a campaign to remove the offending nephew. Reminding the water rat Tommy Squeak of his debt to Mrs. Tubbs, they convince him to call up millions of rats to attack the farm, but the nephew imports three wagon-loads of cats to drive them away. These same cats put an end to a similar attack by masses of swallows. It is only after the dog incites a crowd of wasps to follow him and attack the farm that the nephew flees to London. As in all good folktales, it is the third attempt that is successful. The animals triumphantly lead Mrs. Tubbs back to the farm, where "they never had to leave . . . and they all lived happily ever after" (95).

As with some of the Dolittle tales, the story here has focused on the animals. The title page suggests this emphasis. At first glance, it seems to depict Jip, Gub-Gub, Dab-Dab, Whitey, and Cheapside from Dolittle's animal household, and one could imagine that the story that follows will be one of those told around the Dolittle fireside. But eventually the reader finds that this is the cast of animal characters in the book. Together the dog and pig part the curtain to begin the tale, as though the reader is being invited to a stage play.

The major concern of the novel is kindness repaid, a concern very familiar to readers of the Dolittle series, a concern that is actually central to the Dolittle series. Each of the animals responds because of a prior kindness shown by Mrs. Tubbs. The animals of her household can understand her language not in the same way as in the Dolittle novels but because of their long and happy relationship; they have been her family. When she is in need, the animals respond. "Well, what are we going to do with

the old lady?" (19), asks the dog, his diction indicating the un-
questioned assumption that they are responsible. When the meal
has been prepared, the duck notes that "we must go into the cave
and get a bed ready for Mrs. Tubbs" (25). Now the plot situation
is problematic, since this is the first time a cave has been mentioned and they are in the middle of a wood, but the language
again suggests the assumption of responsibility.

The other two animals react in the same way. The water rat
helps because Mrs. Tubbs once rescued him after he fell into a
bucket of water. "She is the kindest woman to animals in all the
world" (47), he says, and "she certainly ought to be put back on
the farm" (49). The swallow agrees to help because Mrs. Tubbs
once rescued one of her fallen fledglings from a weasel. "We have
got to do our best to . . . put Mrs. Tubbs back in her house, the
same as she put my child back in his nest" (71), she announces to
the gathered swallows. And so, as in *Doctor Dolittle and the Secret Lake,* past acts of kindness are repaid, even from the most
unlikely sources. And the effect of that repayment is the establishment of a home.

The story concludes with the establishment of the home; it is a
conclusion of utter domesticity: "And so when the leaves were all
fallen in the woods, and the trees stood bare waiting for the snow,
they used to sit round the warm fire in the evenings toasting
chestnuts and telling stories while the kettle steamed upon the
hob and the wind howled in the chimney above" (91–95). Reminiscent of the Dolittle friends, this scene evokes images of comfort
and security, images of good things to eat and good stories and
good smells and comforting sounds. It is the home Dolittle seems
always to be searching for but ever uneasy in.

Tommy, Tilly, and Mrs. Tubbs

The sequel to *The Story of Mrs. Tubbs,* unlike that to *The Story
of Doctor Dolittle,* was divided from its predecessor by 13 years;
it was published in 1936. Like its predecessor, it was a hand-size
book, though Lofting drew only a few pictures for it. The title

pages are similar, populated by the three pets of Mrs. Tubbs, and the characters are all the same, with the addition of two children. (Tommy and Tilly in the alliterative title are the water rat and swallow of *The Story of Mrs. Tubbs*.) In short, this novel is a variation on a theme and on a structure, and that variation is only a slight one.

Even the language is reminiscent of the early book. *Tommy, Tilly, and Mrs. Tubbs* opens with a line evoking the season: "One day at the beginning of Summer, when the buds on the hedges had opened into leaf, Mrs. Tubbs was returning from a walk in the woods."[8] This line becomes a refrain used at the end of the book. It recalls a similar line used as a refrain in *The Story of Mrs. Tubbs*: "As the sun was going down behind the little church one evening at the end of Summer when the leaves were beginning to fall in the woods, they all left the farm together" (13). The effect of these repetitions is to bring the two works close together, to make them into a single continuous work, or actually to make one into a repetition of the other. For this is not a sequel in the sense that there is additional growth or added development based on past plot situations. This is the same melody being played in almost the same key.

The structure and plot of the two works are very similar. Where before Mrs. Tubbs had been evicted from her home, here a storm destroys it. Once again she is out in the woods, under the protection of the animals, in search of a home. Sheltering her in the hollow of an oak, the animals again enlist the aid of Tilly the sparrow and Tommy the water rat. Tilly, together with millions of other sparrows, is able to build a house of twigs and leaves around Mrs. Tubbs, but this is destroyed in a subsequent storm. Tommy, however, is able to enlist the aid of other water rats and excavate the cellar of the destroyed house. With the help of two children, a roof is put over the cellar, a hearth is built up, and all is set to rights. It becomes a comfortable, dry, and cozy home.

The reviewer for the *New York Times Book Review* suggested that *Tommy, Tilly, and Mrs. Tubbs* is "another instance of that serious make-believe, that perfectly reasonable and matter-of-fact treatment of nonsense, which delights a youthful audience."[9]

It is indeed this tone that is one of the book's strengths. For non-sense to work, it must not call attention to itself as nonsense; the tone must have a rationality about it that leads to the reader's acceptance of the piece's imaginative context. Both in this story and in *The Story of Mrs. Tubbs,* Lofting achieves that through a neutral narrator who never seems surprised by the events of the plot. And as the narrator perceives these actions, so does the reader in the world Lofting has established; no other perspective is given room.

As in *The Story of Mrs. Tubbs,* kindness is a major concern here. The three pets naturally assume responsibility for Mrs. Tubbs. There are frequent references to the needs of a 100-year-old woman. The animals fend for her, prepare her for the sight of her destroyed home, and warn her of obstacles in a path. The swallows and water rats respond because they recognize that she is the kindest woman in the world. All this mirrors the development of that concern in the first novel.

A new concern here is the character of Pink the pig. In *The Story of Mrs. Tubbs* his role had been very minor: he was a hot water bottle for Mrs. Tubbs's feet. But here he is a pig who has ideas, and though they are disdained by the duck (her relationship to the pig is similar to that of Dab-Dab to Gub-Gub), the reader—and eventually the other animal characters—discover that the pig's ideas have real merit. It is the pig who insists that they dig in the cellar for the Gloucester cheese they use to feed Mrs. Tubbs. He brings the quilt to keep her warm when the animals recognize the inadequacy of leaves. He consults the water rat with the idea of excavating the cellar. He attracts the two children who help to make the cellar into a home.

And so Pink grows up. Whereas before he had been depicted as the irresponsible child, one not allowed to take part in the problem-solving activities of the duck and dog, now he is the one to provide Mrs. Tubbs with a home once again. Where before he was the one who, like Gub-Gub, was concerned only with food, like a child concerned with his own sensory needs, now he is the most thoughtful, reasonable, and innovative of all the animal characters. In the gentle fantasy world of Lofting, the child is given a kind of credence he is rarely accorded. This is the dual element of the delight of this book, and if it is not enough to ensure *Tommy, Tilly, and Mrs. Tubbs* a lasting place in the history of children's literature (it is not), it is at least of interest to a reader of the Dolittle novels, who finds something similar going on in the relationship of Dolittle and Stubbins.

Noisy Nora

Between the two Mrs. Tubbs books, Frederick Stokes published *Noisy Nora,* a slight nonsense tale that parodies and comically undercuts the old-fashioned children's cautionary tale, with its exaggerated emphasis on the effects of a bad habit. Like the Mrs. Tubbs books, *Noisy Nora* was hand-size, though the format was vertical rather than horizontal. Its title page proclaimed that the book was "pictured, told, and printed by Hugh Lofting," and so it was.[10] The text is printed in Lofting's own careful hand, its overlarge size suggesting the careful scribing of a child. The illustrations are a combination of colored drawings and line drawings drawn directly into the text, so that when the narrator notes that Nora's farm has horses and cows and pigs and chickens, small pictures of those animals appear next to the words. Lofting uses this text to suggest the cook's swift movement and the lingering feel of the wind. Together these elements—the size, the printing, and the line drawings—create a look that simulates a child's own production.

The title is once again alliterative, and this, together with the form of the title, suggests that what follows will be a nonsense tale. The adjective linked to a name recalls the taunt of a playmate, and indeed it is a taunt, attached to an ill-behaved girl. That she is "noisy" implies that she may be naughty but is not particularly terrible. Again, it is the kind of title a child might apply. The overwhelming sense this leads to is that the book is as much by a child as it is about a child. It is as if the author has gone beyond looking at situations from a child's-eye view; the author has penetrated into the very world of the child and begun

serving maids in the kitchen.
But she only took one meal there. At luncheon time the cook came to see

scarecrow. And then the worms, peeping from their holes in the ground, noticed there were no birds abroad. And they crept forth to take the air. Not

not to examine it but to participate in it. It is the incalculable limitations imposed by such a stance that makes this only a light tale.

The story begins with a detailing of Nora's neighborhood: she is an ill-mannered eater. She uses her hands (her neighbors are glad she has only two), she keeps her mouth open, and she makes a terrible noise. Unable to endure the noise any longer, her family sends her to eat with the servants. But they too are unhappy, and so Nora is sent to eat with the horses and, upon their complaints (for there is animal language in this book as well), she goes to the cows and then the pigs. When the pigs complain about her messiness, she is sent to an abandoned barn. But there the rats complain, and so her father fences her in at the top of a high hill. On hearing her eat, the wild animals and birds flee, and even the insects hide away. Everything becomes very still, and in that silence Nora hears herself. Abashed, she decides to adopt new manners and goes down with her father to the house in the hollow of the hills, where they all live happily ever after. (Like the Mrs. Tubbs books, this too opens and closes with the conventional folktale lines.)

The subtitle of *Noisy Nora* is "An Almost True Story," and the "almost" is significant in understanding Lofting's conception of the book. He has simply exaggerated to an absurd point a very common experience of childhood: eating with one's mouth open. It is this exaggeration that leads to the nonsense quality of the book, and the nonsense lies in both the plot situations and the language. In terms of the former, Nora is disdained by increasingly low and grubby creatures; Lofting moves from horses to cows to pigs to rats and finally to earthworms. By the end of the book the whole world—even the wind—has gone silent in response to her noise. In terms of the latter, Lofting uses language again to establish a hyperbolic sense of Nora's noise: "Some people said it sounded like a seal coming up for air; others that it reminded them of the sea breaking against the rocks on a stormy night; others said that if they shut their eyes they would think it was a herd of cattle tramping home through the mud" (7–8). That these sounds are very different is irrelevant; it is their exaggerated quality that makes them appropriate for the book.

Like the Mrs. Tubbs books, *Noisy Nora* has gone the way of all insignificant literature. It's chief interest today lies in its being a minor work by a major author of children's literature. Showing none of the whimsy, humor, or charm of the nonsense in the Dolittle books, it can hardly be said to add to Lofting's reputation, and the words "in spite of" spring to mind.

The Twilight of Magic

In 1930 J. B. Lippincott Company published *The Twilight of Magic*; interrupting the great flood of Dolittle books, it was to be unlike anything else Lofting published. On the one hand, it was to be an explicit rejection of the nonsense worlds of Noisy Nora, Gub-Gub, and Mrs. Tubbs. The tone of the narrative is unremittingly serious, and at times even grave. Yet the consideration of nonsense is at the very heart of this novel, for its major concern is a definition of what true sense is. It is the tension between nonsense and sense—later sharpened into a tension between ignorance and prejudice versus tolerance and right reason—that gives this book its dramatic power. Perhaps it is this power that has led to *The Twilight of Magic*'s being one of the two minor works to be reprinted (the other being *The Story of Mrs. Tubbs*).

The Twilight of Magic is the only Lofting book to be illustrated by someone other than the author himself. Lois Lenski, a prominent illustrator during the 1930s, did all of the drawings and included a note describing the delays and hasty writing of the manuscript. Lofting himself seems to have chosen Lenski, for he met with her to describe the early chapters of the book. She was a not-unlikely choice, for though her drawings are much stiffer and more formal than Lofting's, she shared his experience with pen-and-ink drawings. *The Twilight of Magic* was to be "a serious medieval story of two children who have rather mystical experiences," he told her.[11] Given that his own drawings would inevitably be linked to the humorous and fanciful, a result of the popularity of the Dolittle series, Lofting was almost forced to turn to another illustrator if he wished the tone of the illustrations to match the tone of the text.

Reprinted from *The Twilight of Magic* (123) by Hugh Lofting, illustrated by Lois Lenski. Copyright 1930 by Hugh Lofting. Used by permission of Christopher Lofting.

In the short foreword to the 1967 reprint edition of *The Twilight of Magic,* Christopher Lofting defines the novel as "classical fantasy" (4). He is not quite clear what he means by this, but apparently he uses it to separate fantasy novels of high improbability from those of low improbability. (That he lists the Doctor Dolittle books as ones of low improbability suggests something about his assessment of the categories, but the distinction is still a valid one.) *The Twilight of Magic* is a classical fantasy in this sense: that it uses elements of magic to significantly advance the narrative movement of the novel.

Still, the term *classical* is odd in this context, seeming to place *The Twilight of Magic* in the same arena as *Alice in Wonderland, The Wind in the Willows,* or *Peter Pan and Wendy.* It is not among the great fantasies. Perhaps it is truly classical in that it participates in the use of a setting that is so common as to be almost archetypal: the pseudomedieval setting. Lofting told Lenski that he wished this to be "a serious medieval story"; in fact, it is not medieval at all—any more than the folktales of Cinderella, Hansel and Gretel, Rapunzel, and Tom Tit-Tot are medieval. Like those folktales, *The Twilight of Magic* takes place in that timeless world of once-upon-a-time, where characters seem to live in cottages and castles, wear flowing clothes that look somewhat medieval, and still believe there are more things in heaven and earth than are dreamed of in twentieth-century rationalism. If there is anything truly medieval about the novel, it is the tension between the growth of science and conservative philosophical positions. But here too what is a complex of interweaving beliefs in the medieval era is reduced to folktalelike simplicity.

Like some of the Dolittle novels, *The Twilight of Magic* is divided into two parts. In the first, Giles and Anne worry over the financial woes of their father, who is close to losing everything he has. They enlist the aid of Agnes the Applewoman, whom most refer to as Shragga the Witch. She gives them a wonderful shell that, when it grows hot, allows the holder to listen to anyone speaking about him or her. Unsure what to do with it, and afraid lest its discovery might lead some to accuse Agnes of witchcraft, they approach people they trust to ask advice on how it might be used. But it only brings sadness. For Michael the blindman, it brings the knowledge that no one ever thinks of him. For Johannes the philosopher, it brings the news that his ideas are mocked by other philosophers. For Luke the lame boy, it brings reinforcement of his isolation in the town.

The shell seems to invoke a magic world, for as the children leave Luke they stop at a deserted inn. While playing there, a storm comes up and a knocking sounds at the door. As they open it, an elegant woman with her servants enters—the suggestion is that this is Agnes—and the inn is transformed into a comfortable, fecund hostel, with fires blazing in all the rooms. Giles and Anne truly become innkeepers for the night, but when morning comes it all disappears.

Meanwhile, Luke has developed a plan for using the shell: he thinks it should be sold to the new young king. When the king visits the town and arranges a hunting party, Giles boldly steps in front of his horse and holds out the shell. The king is startled but intrigued. He listens to the shell, and then commands Giles to accompany him as the party rides out of the city. Soon he discloses that he had heard Godfrey, the duke of the city, plotting against him, and so the small party flees away to the capital. When he returns—with Giles and with an army—the fleeing Godfrey is killed. For his service Giles is knighted and appointed as the King's Finder. He is brought to court—Anne will follow some years later—and his parents are given sufficient money to be free from all debt.

This ends the first and longer part of the novel. The second is set some years later, and its subject matter is quite different. In fact, it is hardly of a piece with the first half, so radical is the change in setting, plot concerns, and characters. The only consistent element is Agnes, who remains mysterious and evasive. Clearly there is no unity in the plot situations. What does tie the novel together is the common concern of the two halves: the twilight of magic.

At the capital Giles is appointed to wait on the king and to search out things that have been lost. Giles is remarkably adept at this and soon becomes a favorite of the king—a status that carries with it attendant enemies. The secret of the shell is kept, and the king uses it to find traitors. Soon he learns that he can trust no one; his only true friends are Giles and Luke. Eventually he becomes so discouraged that he throws the shell out of a window; Giles retrieves it but gives it to the Queen Mother, Sophronia, who listens to hear herself flattered.

During his time at the castle Giles comes to recognize that he has fallen in love with the Countess Barbara. He is more than a little disappointed, then, when he hears that she has become engaged to the king. Yet just before the wedding she disappears. The king sends his Finder to discover her and to bring her back, and Giles goes out to perform this difficult task. Using the magic shell, he finds her just before she enters a convent; he hides his love for her and brings her back, only to find on his return that the king has fallen and is in danger of losing his life. All is resolved, however, when Agnes mysteriously returns. She restores the king and reveals to him that Giles and Barbara are in love. The king agrees to their marriage, and with joy Giles and Barbara rush to find Agnes. But, as the novel concludes, "Agnes was gone" (303).

Reviews of the novel were cool. "Nothing about this story is as convincing as Dr. Dolittle and his animal friends, nor do the two children, Agnes the Applewoman and the other characters in this new volume ever come very much alive," observed Anne Eaton for the *New York Times Book Review*.[12] In the *Saturday Review of Literature* Laura Benet likened the novel to "the sharp, crisp taste of a fresh ginger cooky [that] becomes slightly flat when it is set too quickly by a window where a breeze is blowing."[13] Both acknowledged that this was a highly imaginative work but argued that the two halves seemed to clash, and that the humor and whimsy of Lofting's other novels were missing here. Certainly Lofting would have replied that he intended those qualities to be missing, and perhaps it is the case that the reviewers wanted the novel to be something it was not meant to be. But in striving for a serious tone, Lofting gave up his greatest literary strength: his infusion of charm, delight, and humor into every conceivable situation.

Yet the reviewers did not acknowledge the generally high quality of Lofting's plotting. At times his tone is just right, as when he depicts the mysterious transformation of the inn, the suspenseful night ride of Giles as he searches for Barbara, or the eerie disappearance of Agnes at the end of the novel. His plotting can be rapid and even breathtaking in its pace, as in the first three dramatic chapters, which introduce the possibility of the supernatural to Giles and Anne. His characterization can be acute, as he develops the close friendship of Luke and Giles. And at times his sentence structures can mirror and emphasize the plot situations, as when the king realizes that his uncle is plotting against him: "At the beginning the king's face had only showed eager, smiling interest, almost like a boy trying a new toy to see if it would work. But as Giles watched, he saw many new expressions pass across it: first a sudden puzzled frown; then, more slowly, a look of horror that changed to anger; next a great sadness, a bereft, almost lonely disappointment; and at last a strange ageing, a hardening, as though in a few moments this gay handsome youth had grown much, much older" (127). The final clause is not strictly necessary, having already been implied, but the rest of the passage, its quick movement emphasized by short, parallel phrasing, is a deft and concise handling of a complicated narrative moment.

The difficulty with this novel is that none of these strengths are sustained. Perhaps this is due to the hasty writing of the book, but in the end a novel must be judged on its final form, and Lofting is never able to consistently develop these strengths. The result is that the characters remain flat, the settings conventional, the plotting at times predictable.

A number of moments in *The Twilight of Magic* recall some of the concerns of the Dolittle novels. "This money business seems a curse, I wish people could live without it altogether" (12), laments Giles in a comment Dolittle himself might have made. Speaking of Geoffrey the Gipsy, the narrator notes that he "was a great enemy of War. And he was always looking forward to the day when it and its unjust evils should pass from the world forever" (187). This sentiment, echoed in the thoughts of Dolittle and

Mudface the Turtle and Pippinella and other Dolittle characters, is repeated when the narrator notes that by listening to the shell, the king could understand the causes of war, could begin to see the other side of an argument and, knowing that other side, could become a preventer rather than a wager of war—a thinly veiled suggestion by Lofting.

Perhaps the image most strikingly connected to the Dolittle books is that of the peaceable Geoffrey, who, interestingly enough, does what Dolittle yearns to do: work in a garden. When Giles takes the shell from him to bring it to Sophronia, he notes Geoffrey's true stature: "But as he looked back, that peaceful figure delving in the earth about the roses suddenly seemed to grow and grow against the sky—taller, stronger and more lasting than the towering castle itself. And when he put the shell in his pocket and turned to go on, Giles knew in his own heart that he was really taking it from the greatest to the smallest" (203). At this moment Giles has an accurate vision of the source of true merit and honor; it comes from one's character. (One is reminded here of Dolittle's preference for cross-bred dogs rather than aristocratic purebreds.) And it is the gardener and the lover of all things peaceful that is more permanent than all the posturings of those around him. Dolittle would not have failed to agree.

But this is not a Dolittle book; nor is there a character quite like Dolittle in it. The reader is in the timeless world of the folktale. Unlike Stubbins, Giles and Anne have no constant mentor; Agnes disappears too often to be a true mentor. The children are for the most part alone, wandering like Hansel and Gretel, but in a city rather than a wilderness. The children, like most folklore children, are not nearly as self-conscious as Stubbins about the meaning of events; they are acted upon by events and characters that seem always just a bit beyond their control. And like folklore children, their rise in the world comes about as goodness and innocence are rewarded, despite all obstacles. That Giles rises to become a favorite of the king is the very stuff of folklore. It is not the stuff of a Dolittle novel.

Lofting perceived the connections of *The Twilight of Magic* to folklore, and perhaps to distance it—in his own mind, he still was writing a medieval tale—he included some metafictive moments in the novel. When the children face the dilemma of how to use the Whispering Shell to bring wealth to their father, Anne remarks, "So it often happens in fairy stories—that great fortune comes from the last place to be expected" (48). When Giles asks for Midnight, the king's horse, as a reward, the king notes that "I would sooner you had asked me for half my kingdom and a princess, the way they do in the fairy tales" (140–41). And when Anne wishes to meet Agnes again so that she could explain the secrets of the Whispering Shell, Giles laments, "People in fairy stories never tell you much" (66). In fact, all three of the metafictive comments are accurate observations about what goes on in this novel: wealth does come from an unexpected source, Giles will ask for a princess, and Agnes will remain enigmatic. Even in distancing the tale from folklore, the metafiction reaffirms its folkloric status, perhaps even unintentionally.

But the major theme of *The Twilight of Magic* would be unusual in a folktale: the tolerance of thought. For Lofting, the medieval period represented a time of intolerance, though certainly intolerance is hardly unique to a culture or time. In this novel the world of the children is on the edge of scientific awareness, and that edge cuts two ways. It destroys fear of the unknown, ignorance of the natural world, and foolish superstition. But it also destroys any notions of magic, that this is a world fraught with power and beauty and mystery that could at any splendid moment break into the life of a character. It is both a twilight and a dawning, and in that equivocal, unsure, intermittent time, Lofting calls for a virtue he had called for before: understanding.

The note is sounded early in the novel. When Anne wonders why people are afraid of Agnes, Giles replies, "I don't believe they know themselves. They don't understand her, I reckon. People are nearly always afraid of what they can't understand—except the very brave ones, maybe" (4). It is a sentiment well beyond the years of this character, but it sets up this theme for the remainder of the book, in which again and again people fear what they do not understand. "That's the way with most fears: they are always fears about what you don't know" (80), remarks Giles.

In general, people in the world of *The Twilight of Magic* are limited by their fears and lack of understanding. They threaten Agnes because of her knowledge of herbs; Johannes, because of his knowledge of chemical properties. The rejection of under-standing—the paralysis of fear—leads to a rejection of both sci-ence and magic: their world is limited indeed. "Anything new!—That's what they're afraid of. They want to make the world stand still. Sometimes I believe they'd sooner see it go backwards rather than forwards" (55), exclaims Johannes.

Lofting has his characters call for tolerance for both worlds of magic and science, though he is concerned not so much with the issue as with the state of mind that breeds intolerance. Against that state of mind he poses characters who humbly accept points of view without reacting with irrational rejections. When Johan-nes can explain the Whispering Shell through neither magic nor science, he notes that "the greatest thinkers have warned us not to be proud of our little knowledge" (61). When Giles asks Geof-frey whether he believes in magic, he replies that he does, "if by that you mean, Sir, anything we can't understand or explain. But don't forget a whole lot passes for magic with us which is simple enough to birds and beasts. Every day something we thought had the Devil in it is shown to be naught more than our own simple-minded ignorance. 'Must be Magic' says Man, as soon as he grows tired of trying to understand a thing. Like children! What's more magic than the way a flower grows out of a seed, I'd like to know?" (198–200). It is the final question that speaks to the novel's theme. In a world filled with wonders, it is naive, dangerous, in-tolerant, and arrogant to assume unquestioningly a particular po-sition. It is a world filled with many kinds of magic, and Lofting calls for his readers to be tolerant of other manifestations of how that magic is embodied.

It is this truth that Giles learns by the end of the novel. While searching for Lady Barbara, Giles wishes for some magic, some wizard to guide him in his search. When none is forthcoming, he laments the passing of magic from the world (this despite his holding the Whispering Shell). But then he looks over the horizon at a spectacular sunset and recognizes that it too is magical:

Gorgeous colors, violet, rose and silver-grey, moving, changing, mingling aswirl. The day of Mystery, wonder stuff and witchcraft, of elves and goblins, jinns and mermaids, fading into quiet dark like the peaceful sleepy ending of enchanted dreams.

Was it the Twilight of Magic? Perhaps. But only today's. Magic could never die while the sun had the power to rise again and Man had the wish to seek. (239–240)

The tremendous affirmation of the narrator in turn affirms the novel's theme of tolerance and understanding. In the face of such continuing mystery, the only proper response is awe and tolerance. Any other is mere nonsense.

6

Conclusion:
The Embattled World of Doctor Dolittle

At the end of *Doctor Dolittle's Return,* Stubbins and Matthew Mugg look up to Dolittle's study to see him working on the problems of time and everlasting life and the tensions that beset the world. It is an image that may be emblematic of the entire Dolittle series: the Doctor, seated under a lamp well into the night, trying to set the world to rights, to bring the kindness that envelops his own life to the rest of the world. It is a quiet, static image, perhaps opposed to the images of the early books, which are dominated by scenes of action and adventure: chasing after slavers, clambering into the Great Sea Snail, meeting Otho Bludge, escaping from various and sundry prisons, tossing a seal over the seaside cliffs. As the series progressed, the images moved from the kind of active ones seen throughout *The Voyages of Doctor Dolittle* to the more static ones of *Doctor Dolittle's Return* and *Doctor Dolittle and the Secret Lake,* as the Doctor became less and less a figure of mere adventure and more and more a figure of social and political reform.

For the child reader, who does not necessarily read the novels through with a sense of chronology (in fact, there is no true chronology in the series as a whole), this change is not particularly significant. That it follows the pattern of Lofting's own life is perhaps even less significant. What is significant is that Dolittle is an evocative, imaginative, adventuresome character; he is a man who can talk to animals, an imaginative leap of pure, delightful, childlike fantasy that allows all of the adventures of the 12 novels to occur.

When Hugh Walpole labeled *The Story of Doctor Dolittle* as a children's classic, he was right, though not in the sense he intended. These novels are not in the same category as *The Wind in the Willows* or *Alice in Wonderland,* if one is to argue on literary grounds alone. They are, however, in the same class in terms of the creation and use of an imaginative context that informs the plot situations of the novels. And they are in the same class in terms of characterization; indeed, it could be argued with some justification that Dolittle and Stubbins are both more finely crafted characters than Alice herself, who always remains the elusive and somewhat mysterious and foreign stuff of a dream. Dolittle and Stubbins are as real as a cup of tea, as familiar as one's favorite toy, as close and good as an afternoon of barefoot fishing.

When the child reader remembers Dolittle's adventures—and this is generalizing, though it seems that an abundance of anecdotal evidence could be marshaled to substantiate the claim—what that reader remembers is Dolittle himself in the midst of the action. At the heart of the imaginative context is the man who can talk to animals. And as a character, he is immensely appealing, not only because of his linguistic gifts but because of his essential kindness. He affords homes to the animals. He finds a preventive for fox hunting. He rescues a circus seal and canaries and dogs penned up in loathsome pet shops. He buys a farm for an aged horse. He travels to Africa to minister to a troupe of monkeys. There is no novel where this quality is not central to Dolittle's character.

He is all the more appealing because the child reader frequently sees him through the eyes of Stubbins. Stubbins is himself struck by the way in which Dolittle treats him, establishing an instant accord by treating him as an equal, by referring to him as Stubbins. In fact, Dolittle is here recognizing that the childlike is not to be despised. (Lofting himself would warn against the loss

of the childlike in the adult).[1] It is to be respected, and even clung
to. It is a respect that does not escape the young reader.

The result is that Dolittle is indeed the stuff of a classic, though
the novels themselves might not be classic in the sense Walpole
means.

In recent years the Dolittle novels have come under attack, an
attack that has led to changes in the text and illustrations of the
Dolittle books. The objections are principally leveled at *The Story
of Doctor Dolittle, The Voyages of Doctor Dolittle,* and *Doctor Dolittle's Post Office,* those novels which involve journeys to Africa.
In those novels, the criticism suggests, Bumpo is caricatured so
grotesquely that the character becomes offensive. Comments by
Linda K. Peterson and Marilyn Leathers Solt are typical: "In
spite of its many merits, the book [*The Voyages of Doctor Dolittle*]
has been less praised in recent years because of the depiction of
Bumpo. After reading the initial description of him, the reader is
certain the author intends to make him a buffoon. . . . The idea of
his being made into a clown is reinforced when one observes that
his speech is filled with long words, frequently incorrectly
used. . . . Although it is not likely the author intended to malign
blacks, it is well that the offensive terms have been deleted from
recent printings."[2] Peterson and Solt go on to defend Bumpo by
noting that his true worth is soon proved. A less equivocal voice
is that of D. Chambers, who argues that Bumpo is "one of the
cruelest stereotypes in the realm of children's literature." The
early Dolittle books, it is argued, have "a nakedly racist message
to offer. A message that clearly states that being white is defi-
nitely an advantage over being black, and that Africans, at least
in this story, are stupid, unaware, and are present only to be
taken advantage of."[3] Isabelle Suhl preferred to attack ad homi-
nem: Lofting "was a white racist and chauvinist, guilty of almost
every prejudice known to modern white Western man."[4]

Certainly there is some material in the Dolittle books that
might cause offense in a contemporary novel. Polynesia uses the
terms *nigger* and *darkie,* and her imprecations against Africa and
its people are bitter and angry. Bumpo is portrayed as a man
yearning to become white, and he and his family are fooled rather

easily because of this yearning and their superstition. And Dolittle does seem to come as the eminent Victorian arriving to Britainize the crude villages of Africa. No matter how well Bumpo is portrayed later on—and in the later books he is a noble and a good figure—he cannot escape this early characterization. The early picture of Bumpo is grotesque in its exaggeration and condescension, though it is well to remember that this kind of exaggeration is common to all of Lofting's early drawings, especially those of Dolittle himself.

The presence of such material has led to various attempts to change the text of the novels. In the fifty-second reprinting of *The Story of Doctor Dolittle*, "darkies" was replaced by "people" and "work with niggers" by "work hard." In *Doctor Dolittle: A Treasury*, published in 1967, Olga Fricker solved the problem simply by not anthologizing those portions of the early novels which contained the offensive depictions. More recently, Dell Publishing has edited eight of the Dolittle novels[5] and published them in what it terms a Centenary Edition. Here those illustrations depicting Africans have been removed, even when such an illustration occurs in the title page. Scenes have been rewritten, so that the chapter in *The Story of Doctor Dolittle* entitled "The Black Prince" is now entitled "The Prince." Where before Bumpo is induced to let Dolittle and his company out of prison in exchange for becoming white, now Polynesia hypnotizes him into freeing them all. It is less offensive, but not a felicitous scene.

In an afterword to the revised novels, Christopher Lofting argues that changing the novels might represent to some a kind of censorship, but "then again, so could a decision to deny access to an entire series of classics on the basis of isolated passing references."[6] He goes on to suggest that Lofting himself would undoubtedly have applauded these changes. While this does not suggest why the editors choose to alter the appearance of Dolittle—does a child demand that he be absolutely consistent?—it does suggest reasons for dropping the offensive passages.

Reviewers of the new series universally welcomed the changes. Selma Lanes, writing in the *New York Times Review of Books*, was typical. She notes that "happily, none of this well-intended edi-

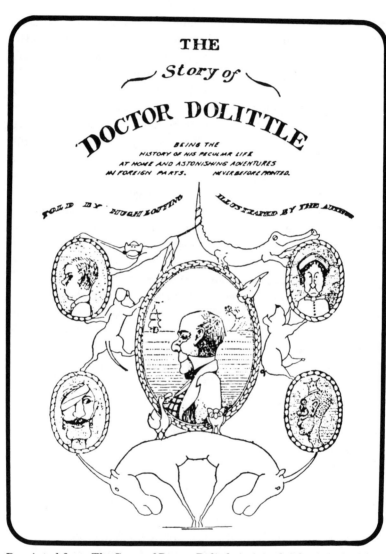

Reprinted from *The Story of Doctor Dolittle* (original title page) by Hugh Lofting. Copyright 1920 by Hugh Lofting. Used by permission of Delacorte Press, a division of Bantam Doubleday Dell Publishing Group, Inc.

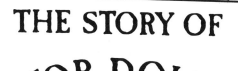

THE STORY OF

DOCTOR DOLITTLE

*Being the
History of His Peculiar Life
at Home and
Astonishing Adventures in Foreign Parts.
Never Before Printed.*

**TOLD BY
HUGH LOFTING**

**ILLUSTRATED BY
THE AUTHOR**

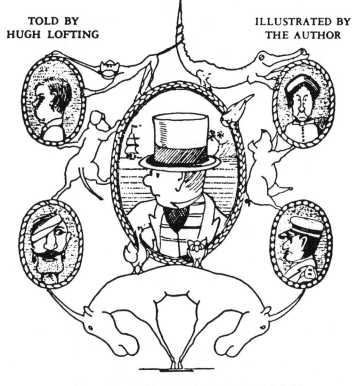

**THE CENTENARY EDITION
DELACORTE PRESS**

torial tinkering has had the slightest effect on the tales' enduring charms. . . . Those of us who loved Doctor Dolittle as children cannot help but wish him well in this slightly tardy centenary appearance."[7] No questions were raised as to the validity of these changes: it was assumed by reviewers that to change the texts was a legitimate process.

Now certainly on one level it is a pleasure to see these passages gone; at times they were gratuitous and offensive. It seems unlikely that this kind of broad caricature would appear in a modern work of children's literature. But on another level these changes—and all the changes made since the fifty-second printing—are problematic. Certainly a modern reader would object to the deleted passages should they appear in a new text, but just as certainly these passages are part of a literary and artistic text. To change them is necessarily to change the text. It will do no good to claim that Lofting himself would have approved; he is not here to change the text, and it stands or falls on its own as a work that comes out of a specific historical context. It is within the historical context that the use of these works and scenes has to be understood.

Now this is an old argument, applied most frequently to *The Adventures of Huckleberry Finn.* It is disturbing, however, when reviewers suggest that children's literature can and should be more readily changed to adapt to the times, that changes may be made so that the books will be more accessible to modern children. Just at a time when children's literature is coming to be taken seriously as literature, this is tiresome. It means that the children's novel is subject to the changing standards of its audience, and that those standards may dominate the integrity of the text. In fact, it means that the text has no internal integrity, for it is constantly up for grabs. One can hardly imagine a similar kind of editorial process in the modern era for, say, *Robinson Crusoe, Moby-Dick,* or *Heart of Darkness,* but a work of children's literature, seemingly, because it is for a child audience, has no similar textual integrity.

Just as disturbing, however, is the assumption that in changing a text, one does not change any of the meaning of the work. When Selma Lanes suggests that there are no significant changes in the novels, she is quite simply wrong. The character of John Dolittle is defined as much by the characteristics he possesses as through opposition. It is a fact rarely noted by critics of the Dolittle novels that Dolittle himself is very rarely liable to the claim of racism. Almost all the racial epithets come from the mouth of Polynesia, and it might be argued with some justice that Lofting is here merely establishing a persona. Even Dolittle's pose of bringing civilization to the dark continent is in fact an attempt to establish order in the only way Dolittle knows. Today it is seen to be ethnocentric, but it seems hardly just to insist on a modern vision of ethnocentrism in a novel written soon after World War I.

In any case, the character of Dolittle is lessened by the changes. Seen against the background of Polynesia's swearing and racial slurs as well as the imagery of the illustrator himself, Dolittle stands in opposition both to the other characters and even to the artist as the single character who insists on respect for all. Certainly this is clear in regard to the animal world, but it is less clear now in regard to the human world. The opposition having been cut, Dolittle's own vision of racial equality is murkier, and actually hardly an issue at all anymore. The cutting has made him blander.

In short, where the novels have lost their objectional passages, they have also lost their historical context, their textual integrity, and their keen portrayal of Dolittle's belief in human equality. This writer, at least, is not so sure that the trade-off has been valuable.

If the Dolittle novels survive as more than mere historical artifacts—and one feels certain they will—it will be because they have triumphed over neglect, acerbic criticism, heavy editing, and silly films through their original wit, humor, and playfulness. Perhaps Lofting's greatest strength was his ability to have Dolittle carry so much so unobtrusively. In the midst of the most remarkable adventures there is gentleness and kindness hardly matched anywhere in children's literature. And there is the plea for tolerance and understanding that comes out of that kindness, a plea that never becomes didactic but is an integral part of the plot situations of the novels.

And there is domesticity, the sense that in the end, one should return to one's own home, one's own garden. At the conclusion of *The Voyages of Doctor Dolittle,* after an astonishing set of adventures, including sinking islands, shipwrecks, battles, and a trip on the ocean floor, Dolittle reaches the shore near Puddleby-on-the-Marsh. "You know, there's something rather attractive in the bad weather of England—when you've got a kitchen-fire to look forward to," he says. "Four o'clock! Come along—we'll just be in nice time for tea" (364). This is the world of Doctor Dolittle: the most ordinary after the most remarkable, the most domestic scene after the most exotic scene, a peaceful kitchen fire after being crowned a king. In the end, this may be Lofting's greatest legacy to his child readers.

Notes and References

Chapter One

1. Colin Lofting, "Mortifying Visit from a Dude Dad," *Life,* 30 September 1966, 128–30.

2. Edward Blishen, *Hugh Lofting* (London: Bodley Head, 1968), 11.

3. Elizabeth Lofting Mutrux, personal interview, 14 May 1990.

4. Cited in Blishen, *Hugh Lofting,* 10.

5. Christopher Lofting, personal interview, 23 May 1990.

6. This was written by Lofting in 1934. It is reprinted in *The Junior Book of Authors,* 2d ed., revised (New York: H. W. Wilson, 1951), 198–99.

7. Christopher Lofting, personal interview, 23 May 1990.

8. Elizabeth Lofting Mutrux, personal interview, 14 May 1990.

9. Colin Lofting, personal interview, 24 May 1990.

10. Christopher Lofting, personal interview, 23 May 1990.

11. Christopher Lofting, personal interview, 23 May 1990.

12. "Children and Internationalism," *Nation,* 13 February 1924, 172–73.

13. Olga Fricker, personal interview, 4 May 1990.

14. Christopher Lofting, personal interview, 23 May 1990.

15. Colin Lofting, personal interview, 24 May 1990.

16. Blishen, *Hugh Lofting,* 18.

17. Both G. Wren Howard and Olga Fricker are cited in Blishen, *Hugh Lofting,* 18.

18. Lois Lenski, "A Note from the Illustrator," in *The Twilight of Magic,* by Hugh Lofting (New York: J. B. Lippincott, 1930; "Note," 1967), vii.

Chapter Two

1. Cited in Roger Lancelyn Green, *Tellers of Tales* (London: Edmund Ward, 1946), 247.

2. Mabel H. B. Mussey, review of *The Story of Doctor Dolittle, Nation,* 6 December 1922, 620.

3. Review of *The Story of Doctor Dolittle, New York Times Book Review,* 12 December 1920, 9.

4. Anne Carroll Moore, review of *The Story of Doctor Dolittle, Bookman,* November 1920, 260.

5. Review of *The Story of Doctor Dolittle, Literary Digest,* 4 December 1920, 89.

6. Green, *Tellers of Tales,* 247.

7. Margaret Blount, *Animal Land: The Creatures of Children's Fiction* (New York: William Morrow, 1975), 199.

8. Helen Dean Fish, "Doctor Dolittle: His Life and Work," *Horn Book,* September–October 1948, 339–46.

9. Edward Blishen, *Hugh Lofting* (London: Bodley Head, 1968), 19.

10. *The Story of Doctor Dolittle* (New York: Frederick Stokes, 1920), 1. Hereafter page references to this edition are cited parenthetically in the text.

11. E. H. Colwell, "Hugh Lofting: An Appreciation," *Junior Bookshelf,* December 1947, 149–54.

12. Blishen, *Hugh Lofting.* 23. See also his comments on the illustrations of Dolittle in *The Story of Doctor Dolittle,* 50–51.

13. Wolfgang Schlegelmilch, "From Fairy Tale to Children's Novel," *Bookbird* 4 (1970): 14–21.

14. *The Voyages of Doctor Dolittle* (New York: J. B. Lippincott, 1922). Hereafter page references to this edition are cited parenthetically in the text.

15. Kenneth Grahame, *The Wind in the Willows* (New York: Charles Scribner's Sons, 1908), 155.

16. Frances Hodgson Burnett, *The Secret Garden* (New York: J. B. Lippincott, 1938), 202.

17. A. A. Milne, *The House at Pooh Corner* (New York: E. P. Dutton, 1928), 178.

18. Jane Austen, *Pride and Prejudice* (Boston: Houghton Mifflin, 1956), 181.

19. Humphrey Carpenter, *Secret Gardens: The Golden Age of Children's Literature* (Boston: Houghton Mifflin, 1985), 210.

Chapter Three

1. Olga Fricker, personal interview, 4 May 1990.

2. Margaret Blount, *Animal Land: The Creatures of Children's Fiction* (New York: William Morrow, 1975), 198.

3. Roger Lancelyn Green, *Tellers of Tales* (London: Edmund Ward, 1946), 247.

4. Edward Blishen, *Hugh Lofting* (London: Bodley Head, 1968), 24.

5. Constance Naar, review of *Doctor Dolittle's Post Office, New Republic,* 14 November 1923, 315.

6. Review of *Doctor Dolittle's Post Office, New York Times Book Review,* 11 November 1923, 4.

7. *Doctor Dolittle's Post Office* (New York: J. P. Lippincott, 1923), 3. Hereafter page references to this edition are cited parenthetically in the text.

8. Humphrey Carpenter, *Secret Gardens: The Golden Age of Children's Literature* (Boston: Houghton Mifflin, 1985), 223.

9. *Doctor Dolittle's Circus* (New York: Frederick A. Stokes, 1924), 374–76. Hereafter page references to this edition are cited parenthetically in the text.

10. Review of *Doctor Dolittle's Zoo, New York Times Book Review,* 8 November 1925, 4.

11. *Doctor Dolittle's Zoo* (New York: Frederick A. Stokes, 1925), 45. Hereafter page references to this edition are cited parenthetically in the text.

12. Marcia Dalphin, review of *Doctor Dolittle's Caravan, New Republic,* 10 November 1926, 353.

13. *Doctor Dolittle's Caravan* (New York: J. B. Lippincott, 1926), 18. Hereafter page references to this edition are cited parenthetically in the text.

14. Review of *Doctor Dolittle's Garden, New York Times Book Review,* 13 November 1927, 35.

15. *Doctor Dolittle's Garden* (New York: Frederick A. Stokes, 1927), 1. Hereafter page references to this edition are cited parenthetically in the text.

16. Cited in Blishen, *Hugh Lofting,* 30.

Chapter Four

1. Review of *Doctor Dolittle in the Moon, New York Times Book Review,* 11 November 1928, 26.

2. Review of *Doctor Dolittle in the Moon, Saturday Review of Literature,* 5 January 1929, 578.

3. Roger Lancelyn Green, *Tellers of Tales* (London: Edmund Ward, 1946), 247.

4. *Doctor Dolittle in the Moon* (New York: Frederick A. Stokes, 1928), 264. Hereafter page references to this edition are cited parenthetically in the text.

5. *Doctor Dolittle's Return* (New York: J. B. Lippincott, 1933), 1. Hereafter page references to this edition are cited parenthetically in the text.

6. Edward Blishen, *Hugh Lofting* (London: Bodley Head, 1968), 35.

7. Review of *Doctor Dolittle and the Secret Lake, Atlantic Monthly,* November 1948, 119.

8. Ellen Lewis Buell, review of *Doctor Dolittle and the Secret Lake, New York Times Book Review,* 3 October 1948, 35.

9. *Doctor Dolittle and the Secret Lake* (New York: J. B. Lippincott, 1948), 3. Hereafter page references to this edition are cited parenthetically in the text.

10. Blishen, *Hugh Lofting,* 40.

11. *Doctor Dolittle and the Green Canary* (New York: J. B. Lippincott, 1950), 275. Hereafter page references to this edition are cited parenthetically in the text.

12. Ellen Lewis Buell, review of *Doctor Dolittle and the Green Canary, New York Times Book Review,* 1 October 1950, 24.

13. Jane Cobb, review of *Doctor Dolittle's Puddleby Adventures, New York Times Book Review,* 16 November 1952, 36.

14. *Doctor Dolittle's Puddleby Adventures* (New York: J. B. Lippincott, 1952), v. Hereafter page references to this edition are cited parenthetically in the text.

Chapter Five

1. Edward Blishen, *Hugh Lofting* (London: Bodley Head, 1968), 44.

2. *Gub-Gub's Book: An Encyclopedia of Food in Twenty Volumes* (New York: Frederick Stokes, 1932), title page. Hereafter page references to this edition are cited parenthetically in the text.

3. *Doctor Dolittle's Birthday Book* (New York: Frederick Stokes, 1936), unpaged. Hereafter page references to this edition are cited parenthetically in the text.

4. *Porridge Poetry: Cooked, Ornamented, and Served Up* (New York: Frederick Stokes, 1924), title page. Hereafter page references to this edition are cited parenthetically in the text.

5. Winston Churchill, "Their Finest Hour," in *Blood, Toil, Tears, and Sweat: The Speeches of Winston Churchill,* ed. David Cannadine (Boston: Houghton Mifflin, 1989), 167–78.

6. *Victory for the Slain* (London: Jonathan Cape, 1942), 16. Hereafter page references to this edition are cited parenthetically in the text.

7. *The Story of Mrs. Tubbs* (New York: Frederick Stokes, 1923), 7.

Hereafter page references to this edition are cited parenthetically in the text.

8. *Tommy, Tilly, and Mrs. Tubbs* (New York: Frederick Stokes, 1936), 1. Hereafter page references to this edition are cited parenthetically in the text.

9. Review of *Tommy, Tilly, and Mrs. Tubbs, New York Times Book Review,* 7 March 1937, 10.

10. *Noisy Nora: An Almost True Story* (New York: Frederick Stokes, 1929), i. Hereafter page references to this edition are cited parenthetically in the text.

11. *The Twilight of Magic* (New York: Frederick Stokes, 1930), vii. Hereafter page references to this edition are cited parenthetically in the text.

12. Anne T. Eaton, review of *The Twilight of Magic, New York Times Book Review,* 7 December 1930, 45.

13. Laura Benet, review of *The Twilight of Magic, Saturday Review of Literature,* 15 November 1930, 344.

Chapter Six

1. See "Hugh Lofting," in *The Junior Book of Authors,* 2d ed., revised (New York: H. W. Wilson, 1951), 198–99.

2. Linda Kauffman Peterson and Marilyn Leathers Solt, *The Newbery Medal and Honor Books, 1922–1981: An Annotated Bibliography* (Boston: G. K. Hall, 1982), 15–17.

3. D. Chambers, "How, Now, Dr. Dolittle?" *Elementary English* 45 (April 1968): 437–39, 445.

4. Isabelle Suhl, cited in Selma Lanes, "Doctor Dolittle, Innocent Again," *New York Times Book Review,* 28 August 1988, 20.

5. The eight novels Dell has chosen to republish are *The Story of Doctor Dolittle, The Voyages of Doctor Dolittle, Doctor Dolittle's Circus, Doctor Dolittle's Caravan, Doctor Dolittle and the Green Canary, Doctor Dolittle's Post Office, Doctor Dolittle's Garden,* and *Doctor Dolittle in the Moon.* One can only speculate on why *Doctor Dolittle's Return* was not chosen, given that it is such an immediate sequel to *Doctor Dolittle in the Moon,* or why *Doctor Dolittle and the Secret Lake* and *Doctor Dolittle's Zoo* were omitted. The British publisher Jonathan Cape will be publishing all 12 of the novels in the series. For further information on this series, see Maureen J. O'Brien, "Doctor Dolittle Is Back," *Publishers Weekly,* 26 February 1988, 122, and Lori Mack, "A Publisher's Perspective," *Horn Book,* May/June, 1988, 382–84.

6. Christopher Lofting, afterword to *The Story of Doctor Dolittle,* by Hugh Lofting (New York: Delacorte Press, 1988), 153.

7. Selma Lanes, "Doctor Dolittle, Innocent Again," 20.

Selected Bibliography

Primary Works

Doctor Dolittle: A Treasury. Compiled by Olga Fricker. New York: J. B. Lippincott, 1967.

Doctor Dolittle and the Green Canary. New York: J. B. Lippincott, 1950.

Doctor Dolittle and the Secret Lake. New York: J. B. Lippincott, 1948.

Doctor Dolittle in the Moon. New York: Frederick Stokes, 1928.

Doctor Dolittle's Birthday Book. New York: Frederick Stokes, 1936.

Doctor Dolittle's Caravan. New York: J. B. Lippincott, 1926.

Doctor Dolittle's Circus. New York: Frederick Stokes, 1924.

Doctor Dolittle's Garden. New York: Frederick Stokes, 1927.

Doctor Dolittle's Post Office. New York: J. B. Lippincott, 1923.

Doctor Dolittle's Puddleby Adventures. Edited by Josephine Lofting. New York: J. B. Lippincott, 1952.

Doctor Dolittle's Return. New York: J. B. Lippincott, 1933.

Doctor Dolittle's Zoo. New York: Frederick Stokes, 1925.

Gub-Gub's Book: An Encyclopedia of Food in Twenty Volumes. New York: Frederick Stokes, 1932.

Noisy Nora: An Almost True Story. New York: Frederick Stokes, 1929.

Porridge Poetry: Cooked, Ornamented, and Served Up. New York: Frederick Stokes, 1924.

The Story of Doctor Dolittle. New York: Frederick Stokes, 1920.

The Story of Mrs. Tubbs. New York: Frederick Stokes, 1923.

Tommy, Tilly, and Mrs. Tubbs. New York: Frederick Stokes, 1936.

The Twilight of Magic. Illustrated by Lois Lenski. New York: J. B. Lippincott, 1930.

Victory for the Slain. London: Jonathan Cape, 1942.

The Voyages of Doctor Dolittle. New York: J. B. Lippincott, 1922.

Writings on Children's Literature

"Children and Internationalism." *Nation,* 118 (13 February 1924): 172–73.

"Hugh Lofting." In *The Junior Book of Authors,* 2d ed., revised (New York: H. W. Wilson Company, 1951), 198–99.

Secondary Works

Biographical Studies

Fish, Helen Dean. "Doctor Dolittle, His Life and Work." *Horn Book,* 24 (September–October 1948): 339–46. Written by his editor, the article examines the interrelationships of Lofting's life and work.
———. "Dr. Dolittle's Creator." *Saturday Review of Literature,* 31 (10 January 1948): 28–29. A tribute to Lofting, written after his death, recounting the first meeting of the two and the popularity of the series.
Jones, Mary Elizabeth. "Connecticut's Puddleby-on-the-Marsh." *Horn Book,* 44 (August 1968): 463, 475. A report on a talk by Elizabeth Lofting Mutrux, dealing with the homes the Lofting family inhabited while living in Connecticut.
Lofting, Colin. "Mortifying Visit from a Dude Dad." *Life,* 61 (30 September 1966): 128–30. An anecdote dealing with a visit from Lofting to a ranch.
Shenk, Dorothy. "Hugh Lofting: Creator of Doctor Dolittle." *Elementary English* 32 (April 1955): 201–8. A highly laudatory recounting of Lofting's career, moving through the Dolittle novels as well as some of the minor works.

Critical Studies

Blishen, Edward. *Hugh Lofting.* London: Bodley Head, 1968. This monograph, the longest of the critical studies mentioned here, deals with Lofting's life as well as his work. It includes brief studies of all the Dolittle novels, as well as the minor works, concluding that Lofting's greatest asset was his comic imagination.
Blount, Margaret. *Animal Land: The Creatures of Children's Fiction.* New York: William Morrow, 1975, 198–201. Examines the ways in which the animals of the Dolittle series contribute thematically.
Cameron, Eleanor. *The Green and Burning Tree.* Boston: Little, Brown, 1969, 49–56. In an informal style, criticizes the claim that *The Story of Doctor Dolittle* is a classic and attacks the scientific inaccuracies of the novels.

Chambers, D. "How, Now, Doctor Dolittle?" *Elementary English* 45 (April 1968): 437–39, 445. A bitter, somewhat virulent attack on the Dolittle novels, claiming they are racist.

Colwell, E. H. "Hugh Lofting: An Appreciation." *Junior Bookshelf,* December 1947, 149–54. A highly laudatory and not very scholarly examination of the merits of the Dolittle series, examining those elements which hold the child reader's interest.

Fisher, Margery. *Intent upon Reading.* New York: Franklin Watts, 1962, 62. Examines Lofting's handling of animals, both in the text and in the illustrations.

Green, Roger Lancelyn. *Tellers of Tales.* London: Edmund Ward, 1946, 246–48; reprint, New York: Franklin Watts, 1965. Background and evaluation of the Dolittle series, concluding that the first novel is different in kind from the later books in the series.

Mack, Lori. "A Publisher's Perspective." *Horn Book,* 64 (May/June, 1988): 382–84. Explains the development and purpose of the Delacorte reprinting of the Dolittle series.

Schlegelmilch, Wolfgang. "From Fairy Tale to Children's Novel." *Bookbird* 4 (1970): 14–21. Explains the movement from the first novel to the second as a movement from the motifs of the folktale to the motifs of the fantasy novel.

Schmidt, Gary. "The Craft of the Cobbler's Son: Tommy Stubbins and the Narrative Form of the *Doctor Dolittle* Series." *Children's Literature Association Quarterly* 12 (Spring 1987): 19–23. Explores the narrative implications of Stubbins in *The Voyages of Doctor Dolittle* particularly, focusing on Stubbins as a selective lens.

Film

Doctor Dolittle. Twentieth Century-Fox, 1967.

Index

The Author

Gary D. Schmidt received his B.A. from Gordon College, Wenham, Massachusetts, and his M.A. and Ph.D in medieval literature from the University of Illinois at Urbana-Champaign. An associate professor of English at Calvin College, in Grand Rapids, Michigan, he teaches children's literature, medieval and renaissance literature, and the history of the English language. He is especially interested in the role of the narrator, and has coedited *The Voice of the Narrator in Children's Literature* (1989) and *Sitting at the Feet of the Past: Retelling the North American Folktale* (1992). The author of *Robert McCloskey* (1990) he has also contributed to such journals as *Children's Literature in Education,* the *Children's Literature Association Quarterly, Mediaevalia,* the *Journal of the Rocky Mountain Medieval and Renaissance Association,* and *Concerning Poetry.* He is currently editing the twelfth-century *Vision of the Monk of Evesham,* writing a book on Katherine Paterson, and gathering materials for a biography of St. Bede.